Unseen Horizons

A Blind Man's Story of Grit, Grace and Greatness

Narrated by

Dr. M. V. Shirdhonkar

Transcribed by Daughter

Dr. Jyotsna Sarwaikar

Qurate
qauratebooks.com

UNSEEN HORIZONS

A Blind Man's Story of Grit, Grace and Greatness

Dr. M. V. Shirdhonkar

Published in 2025

© Published by

Qurate
qauratebooks.com

Qurate Books Pvt. Ltd.
Goa 403523, India
www.quratebooks.com
Tel: 1800-210-6527, Email: info@quratebooks.com

ISBN: 978-93-58982-83-1

"O God! Salute to thy supreme power,
It makes dumb to speak,
Crippled to conquer Mount Everest,
Wherever thy blessings are,
There exists everlasting super happiness!"

Dedications

"Victory or death in battle has been the religion of the Rajput from time immemorial. It is his character that he knows no fear."

-Motto of the Rajputs

This autobiography is humbly dedicated to those trainers, parents, siblings and persons with some kind of disability, who struggled and fought for the protection and restoration of their rights, not only in India but across the whole world.

Wars are not only fought along the borders, but are fought within the country too, for the sake of humanity. It is a global war fought for rights of 'Persons with Disability' where the War Heroes often go unnoticed.

Many have selflessly fought in this war, with devotion and dedication, to help humanity, leaving the results in the hands of Almighty God. They are the real warriors – The Rajputs and I salute them as an individual, who himself has gone through a long journey full of pain and dismay.

Contents

Acknowledgement

In this long journey of 83 years, when I look back, I try to visualize how many great souls have helped and inspired me to overcome my blindness, depression, frustration, and limitations, bringing out the creative and resourceful person within me. I sincerely extend my gratitude to all those who joined me along the way, making my life positive, assertive, and fruitful.

First and foremost, I express my gratitude and pay tribute to the Almighty God; without His will, this work would have been impossible. His mercy and blessings are the sole reason for the creation of this work.

I still feel the blessings of my grandparents, parents, uncle, and friends, who have always been with me and have made my life meaningful and worthwhile for society. I marvel at the dual role of nature, which works both negatively and positively side by side, ultimately making us stronger in facing adversities. By taking away my outward eyesight, nature seemed to strip everything from my life; yet, at the same time, it gradually bestowed upon me everything needed to overcome the loss of sight: the darkness of ignorance, social rejection, and other obstacles that kept me from integrating into the mainstream of society. For this, I am deeply grateful to providence, which has so generously brought me to where I stand today with human dignity.

My life took a positive turn when I joined V. M. School for the Blind, Mumbai. The Principal of the school, Lt. Shri. K N K Justawala, was a great teacher and a good human being who had a special place for me in his heart, behavior, and actions. He sincerely believed that I had the inner vision and positive attitude to become a contributory member of society. He was my guru in every respect, and I pay my respects to him every day, even now. I am indeed fortunate that I remained under his guidance for years, shaping my life to the present level. I owe my utmost gratitude to Lt. Rustamji Alpaiwala, the first president of NAB India, and his wife, Mrs. Alpaiwala, who provided me with strong emotional support during my stay in Mumbai and even after I left. I can't forget his humble gesture when he gave me a letter of introduction to his relative in Mhow, who subsequently introduced me to Dr. J. N. Pohawala, a senior pediatrician. Dr. Pohawala and Dr. Chaman Lal Nagrath, an orthopedic surgeon, were generous enough during my initial years to refer cases to me for physiotherapy practice.

Procuring a job in a government hospital for a blind person was almost a dream in the years 1956-57. However, it became a reality due to the generosity and understanding of the then Governor, Lt. Shri. H. V. Pataskar, and the then Hon'ble Chief Minister, Lt. Shri. K. N. Katju. I thus express my heartfelt gratitude to those great souls who came forward with their bold decisions and actions.

When I initiated the formation of the organization for the blind, I received a positive response from a few leading personalities of Indore, such as Shri. Labhchandji Chajlani of Nai Dunia Press, Shri. Chandan Singhji Barkatia, noted social worker and M.D. of Malwa Mills, Lion Mr. Balkrishana Shah, and eminent ophthalmologist Dr. R. C. Dhanda. All of them were generous enough to join me in the formation of the organization. I humbly respect them, and this will forever remain in my mind. A leader alone cannot bring desired outcomes unless a team of dedicated workers joins him with the same vision. Thus, I do not hesitate to gracefully share all achievements so far with all those who joined me in this long journey.

My special thanks go to Dr. J. H. Yadav, Cardiologist, and Dr. K. C. Khare, Consultant Physician, who, over the years, helped me overcome my medical ailments, keeping me fit to contribute my humble services to society. As time passed, a few other senior citizens and noted social workers from the business community also joined the organization at my request and contributed for years to the cause of the blind. Among them, Lt. Shri. Harikishan Muchhal, Shri. Gyanchand Nahar, Shri. Banwarilalji Jaju, and Lion Ratanlal Gupta are a few to whom my profound gratitude stands.

The staff members of the M.P. Welfare Association for the Blind and the M.P. Branch of the National Association for the Blind worked with me with sincerity and dedication for years, and my words of appreciation and blessings for them remain at the core of my heart. I would also like to acknowledge Lt. Col. Dr. V. K. Gautam, President of Parivaar (National Confederation of Parents' Organizations), for editing the work despite his busy schedule as a philanthropist, and Shri. Trivedi for his consistent support in taking the draft of the autobiography.

Nevertheless, I am continually obliged by senior officials of the Indian Administrative Services for their positive approach and decision-making in the larger interest of the visually impaired in Madhya Pradesh. I am hopeful that such awareness will be strengthened and expanded among all bureaucrats who, whenever and wherever they have the opportunity, can be involved in the decision-making process related to the cause of blindness.

Last but not least, my heartfelt gratitude goes to my family—my wife for her untiring and selfless support; my daughter for her intellectual and literary inputs; and my brothers, Shri. Eknath and Shri. Vishwanath Shirdhonkar, for all their gestures that made me strong enough to bring out this piece of work.

Date: 15th Jan, 2016

Place: Indore

(Dr. M. V. Shirdhonkar)

Voices of Appreciation

I feel honored to write a small note for my dear colleague - Dr. M. V. Shirdhonkar.

This book, I experience not only as an autobiography of a blind person, but also as a book describing a journey filled with hardship, full of turbulences with 'pitching and rolling' in the high sea.

Many have a bitter experience of life, especially at an early age, but they learn how to fight this battle single-handedly, against all odds, yet remaining humble.

This piece of autobiography has been written in a very systematic chronological manner. It not only covers the expression of life, professional and social system, but also gives insight and wisdom to the youth regarding how to lead an ideal life with inspiring examples and citations.

I am sure readers will be benefitted and will get encouraged to perform social responsibilities.

(P. K. Pincha)

Chief Commissioner

Ministry of Disability Affairs, New Delhi

***

This autobiography of Dr. M. V. Shirdhonkar, 'Unseen Horizons', narrates the story of a man who transformed his limitations into strengths and achieved great heights both personally and professionally.

Born with extremely weak eyesight, he lost his vision completely at the age of 14. Yet, his commitment was unparalleled, shaping various dimensions of his life.

Dr. Shirdhonkar completed his matriculation in Mumbai and specialized in physiotherapy, typing, and English. After his education, he returned to Indore, earned a Master's degree in Social Science, and began practicing physiotherapy at a government hospital.

Along with other noble citizens of Indore, he took the initiative to establish the Madhya Pradesh Welfare Association for the Blind (MPWAB). Dr. Shirdhonkar strongly believed in the economic rehabilitation of visually challenged individuals and, through this organization, was able to help many. This book details the initiatives of MPWAB, which successfully provided professional technical training and job placements for the blind, among other initiatives. The organization's efforts significantly contributed to infrastructure development for the visually challenged in northern India, with Dr. Shirdhonkar serving as a key catalyst.

His dedication to improving the lives of visually impaired individuals is truly commendable. He empowered them to become independent and successful, enabling them to live with dignity in society.

The publication of this book is a significant milestone—not only for those facing challenges but also for society, reminding us to treat such individuals with the utmost dignity and care.

Nirmala Buch
Former Chief Secretary,
Government of Madhya Pradesh

A Daughter's Gratitude: Words For My Father

Some lives are not just lived; they illuminate the path for others. My father's journey is one such story—a narrative woven with resilience, wisdom, and an unbreakable spirit. His life, though marked by challenges, was never defined by them. Instead, he turned each adversity into an opportunity, each struggle into strength, and each limitation into a new possibility.

From the earliest days of my life, I have witnessed his unwavering determination to rise above circumstances that many would have deemed insurmountable. His physical blindness never hindered his vision for a meaningful life, nor did it deter him from empowering others through his insights, teachings, and service to society. His story is not merely one of overcoming personal struggles but of redefining the very essence of human potential. He showed the world that true vision comes not from one's eyes but from one's heart and mind.

As his daughter, I have been profoundly inspired by his philosophy of life. His teachings instilled in me the values of perseverance, self-belief, and the importance of service to others. He taught me that life is not about what we lack, but about how we use what we have. His conviction that knowledge is not confined to those with perfect eyesight, but is instead an amalgamation of inner vision, wisdom, and experience, is a lesson that will forever resonate with me.

This autobiography is a testament to these beliefs. It is not just a story—it is a guiding light for those who seek inspiration in times of darkness. Through his words, he addresses questions that are not just his own, but those that echo in the hearts of many who grapple with self-doubt and limitations. His reflections challenge societal perceptions, urging us to look beyond physical constraints and recognize the boundless potential within each individual.

While my father narrated his life experiences and reflections, I had the privilege of transcribing his words in the form of this book. This autobiography is a labor of love, a bridge between his voice and the readers who seek inspiration in his journey. It is not just his story; it is a message of hope, an awakening of the human spirit, and a reminder that no obstacle is too great when faced with courage and determination.

It is my deepest honor to present my father's autobiography, expressing my gratitude for a father whose wisdom and kindness have shaped my life and countless others. His life's mission was to uplift, inspire, and redefine possibilities—and through this work, that mission continues.

May his words reach and touch the hearts of all who read them, just as his life has touched mine.

With Love and Reverence,

His Daughter Jyotsna (Mana)

***

Dr. Jyotsna Sarwaikar is a distinguished Development Professional, Mindset and Self-Development Life Coach, Garbh Sanskar Coach, and an Author. Over the past three decades, she has influenced and transformed countless lives. She credits her success to her father Dr. M. V. Shirdhonkar (late), with whom she shared a close bond.

Her father was a living example who instilled in her the values of unwavering resilience and commitment to serve others. Witnessing her father turn adversities into opportunities made her realise that "vision" emerges from within. This guiding principle became the cornerstone of her work in empowering vulnerable individuals such as women trapped in self-doubt, youth seeking direction, specially-abled persons striving to integrate into society and others in need of support.

As a Garbh Sanskar Coach, she nurtures life from its very inception, weaving ancient wisdom with modern insights. Honored with the International Women's Gloriya Award and an honorary doctorate, Dr. Sarwaikar continues to illuminate lives with compassion, wisdom, and transformative guidance.

Preface

"The only thing worse than being blind is having sight but no vision."

-Helen Keller

For many years, I carried the thought of turning my life story into an autobiography. However, a barrage of questions, counter-questions, and doubts often troubled me, making it difficult to make a firm decision. It took time to resolve these inner conflicts, and I had to work within certain constraints to address the issues that held me back from writing. Throughout my life, I have tried to live with a mission to serve society, and this journey has been driven by my pursuit to find answers to the following key questions that have guided my efforts:

1. There are numerous autobiographies of eminent personalities available to readers, so I wondered—what impact would my story, which only narrates the struggles of a visually challenged person, have on them? But then, I realized the answer lay within. I believe this work would not only inspire the visually impaired and disabled individuals

who often survive with minimal community support, but it might also raise awareness and sensitize those 'normal' people who, despite having all the resources, still live with a negative mindset!

2. Do we truly believe that eyesight is the only dominant sense organ in the human body, essential for acquiring knowledge and achieving human perfection? I believe that every individual, whether with or without eyesight, possesses a form of inner vision. This inner vision needs to be explored and harnessed to make each person unique in their own way, ultimately contributing to the well-being of society.
3. I admire all those who, despite living in extreme scarcity, still share their happiness with others and rise above adversities to reach heights that few achieve—unlike those who, despite having more resources, may have lost the will to strive or share with others.
4. I further believe that not only eyesight, but also the residual senses of hearing, touch, taste, and smell, play an effective role in gaining knowledge of the world around us. Twenty vital losses have been narrated by Father Carol, an eminent rehabilitation professional, in relation to the loss of sight among which include: loss of communication, loss of mobility, loss of reading and writing skills, lack of aesthetic sense, and, above all, the loss of the eye is the loss of 'I'. Experience reveals that most of these losses can be coped with through proper training, knowledge, and understanding. A more significant aspect to keep in mind is that the loss of 'I' can only be dealt with through multiple elements of vision beyond eyesight. Eyesight alone doesn't represent 'I', i.e., total personality

development. A vague and unacceptable misconception hampers the all-around development of those who suffer from the loss of sight. All other residual senses equally play an important role in human development, even in the absence of sight. It is, therefore, not correct to say that there is 'no life' without eyesight. People without eyesight must understand, deep in their hearts, that the loss of eyesight is not the end of life. Instead, life should be accepted as a challenge and lived with zeal, to become an inspiration for others.

5. Presently, academic education alone does not lead a person to human perfection. I have tried to visualize human perfection as something that can be achieved even with little or no academic background. Readers may agree that residual senses, mental faculties, and the inner self play major roles in shaping a human being towards perfection on multiple levels. This clearly indicates that knowledge cannot be acquired solely through eyesight; it is also gained through inner strength, willpower, and a positive attitude towards life. One can lead society through their unique contributions by identifying and highlighting new dimensions of inner vision, which serve as a true motivating force.
6. Most of us live our lives focused solely on ourselves, with our interests confined to our family. We rarely think about those around us who are in need of a helping hand. However, a small and timely gesture of assistance to someone in need can become a wonderful contribution to their life. Over time, this act of kindness can inspire hundreds, thousands, and sometimes even all those around us.

7. Last but not the least, it has been practically experienced that light (vision) comes as we work towards it. Thus, while living through the darkness of sight, I gained light (vision) by making every possible effort. It would give me immense pleasure if even one person is inspired to continue their journey with zeal and enthusiasm through this insight and newfound vision.

Dr. M. V. Shirdhonkar

2016

Introduction

"It is the most peculiar subject in nature, but it means much for me and my brother fellows. Therefore, after reading the book, my readers will realize that it means equally to humanity with humility."

-Anonymous

Providence has bestowed abundant potential upon human beings. However, we hardly take stock of such a wonderful gift of nature. Occasionally, we recognize these gifts in the form of physical strength, extraordinary mental faculties, or, rarely, even spiritual strength. Each one of us is unique in our own way and cannot be compared to others in any way. This indicates that every individual has been entrusted with specific responsibilities in life, and Providence enriches them to perform the duties entrusted by nature. It is up to the individual to determine how optimally they utilize these unique abilities in the larger interest of their own well-being and, preferably, the well-being of society.

For quite some time, I have been reminded by a good number of my friends that I should bring out my landmark achievements in the form of an autobiography. I took much time to think over this idea, and now, at the start of the 9th decade of my life, I have finally decided to collect all my old and cherished memories in book form, which may help our younger generation lead society in the years ahead. As mentioned above, I am very conscious of the abundant potential hidden in the youth of our nation. Often, we are afraid of taking on challenges and rarely accept the ones that are forced upon us by nature or otherwise. Since there are abundant challenges in human life, we sometimes get depressed and lose confidence in coping with them. I believe that challenges are our friends and should be seen as steps to climb a ladder to fulfill our dreams. From my own experience, I have found that as we face challenges, we develop the abilities to cope with higher-level challenges, which strengthens our personality and helps us become contributory members of society. I remember the wonderful quotation by the late Minu Masani, which says, "How narrow is the path that leads to life, how broad are the roads that lead to destruction." All of us, therefore, have to work to make the path of life broader and broader at an appreciable level. I read this quotation almost 50 years ago, and since then, my efforts have been directed toward making the path of life broader and broader—not only for myself, but for my fellow beings and society at large.

In my view, it is a difficult task to write about one's own self-accomplishments, rather than writing about the achievements of the people around us, unless inspirations from both outside and within come together and awaken dormant memories, bringing them out in the form of such documents. I fully express my gratitude to Providence for inspiring me to undertake this herculean task of bringing my dormant memories to the forefront in the form of this humble expression.

My life has been full of adversities, challenges, and rejections; nevertheless, it is also full of accomplishments. The latter brings me pleasure, while the former is the garbage that has been left far behind. This has inspired me to take a fresh look at overcoming all possible issues with positive and rational thinking. Gross atrocities, knowingly or unknowingly, were imposed on me by family members, so-called friends, society, and even by nature. However, by taking proper care in coping with the negative attitudes of society, I have worked to make life more positive and meaningful—not only for myself but also for all those who have been victimized by similar atrocities.

While beginning to write this autobiography, a picture of a child "IN THE DUSTBIN" comes to my mind, which moves me to write with the utmost sensitivity, using the words within my command. Occasionally, we observe that human life is treated as if a newborn child is thrown into a garbage bin near a "Mango Tree." A few more people add their garbage to the bin, but none try to bring the child out of it. Then, someone, out of sympathy, rescues the child from the garbage and places him beneath the tree. However, he does not take the child to his family, and raising the child is not at all in his mind. How the child was reared at the mercy of nature, and how, in his youth, he eventually becomes a gardener of a huge, beautiful garden, is beyond normal understanding.

Before I proceed with the other chapters, I would like, with utmost humility, to summarize the basic issues I am going to cover in the succeeding chapters. My life compels me to write about a child without a mother and raised by someone else in the family. Love and hatred went side by side. How such behavior affected the child in both the positive and negative spectrums of life is, again, beyond understanding.

The breadth of blindness destroys the total pattern of existence. The sighted person is lost, and the blind person is born, but there is still life ahead. The major issue that influences me to write further is the belief that if society has something to offer and the blind person is willing to accept it and march from darkness to light, then he becomes a normal person too!

I have realized that people die many times throughout their lifetimes. However, they must reorganize themselves for a new life each time. The sudden death of a loved one, unwanted divorce, unsuccessful love affairs, great financial loss, or any such events can bring us close to suicidal thoughts. One must reorganize themselves to emerge from such mourning and move forward with a positive attitude, determined to conquer something in their own life. Only such a positive attitude can lead one forward; nothing else can help overcome adversity, whether it is imposed upon them by society or caused by a natural calamity. Self-esteem and a strong drive are essential to walking along the narrow path that leads to life.

I would like to emphasize here that atrocity and adversity cannot prevent a person from leading a positive life or cherishing the basic goals of their life. Again, everyone must set an ideal goal to accomplish, consistent with their attitude and a willingness to work hard for it. No one in the world can then prevent them from reaching their desired destination.

All those who, most of the time, approach society with a negative attitude must realize the fact that negative and positive waves move simultaneously, parallel to each other. It is up to the individual to choose whether to take the support of the positive rope to climb to the top of the tree, or to hold the weak rope of negative attitude, which will cause them to collapse in the middle and fall down once and for all. I would like to share that good thoughts bear good fruits, and bad thoughts bear bad fruits. Therefore, do not allow negative or bad thoughts to take shelter in your mind at any moment, no matter the condition.

"Pleasure comes to us as much as we extend it to others who need it the most." It is the nectar of a successful human life. I, even with blindness, have experienced it to a great extent while providing services for the visually impaired and those with associated disabilities over the past 50 years. International personalities like the late Prime Minister, Pandit Jawaharlal Nehru, and the eminent writer, philosopher, and thinker, Dr. Helen Keller, blessed me with the opportunity to serve this noble cause.

***

Chapter 1

Family Ancestry

"If you want to find out the purpose of life, you need to look beyond the limitations of body and mind."

-Sadhguru

Kuladevata

Every family is identified by its own title. All members of a family use this title to signify the family they belong to. In Maharashtra, many families derive their titles from the name of their native place or town. For instance, people from Nasik or those descended from Nasik are recognized as "Nasikkar." Similarly, people originating from Satara and living elsewhere are known as "Satarkar." Our family descended from a small town called "Shirdhon" in the Sangli district, and thus, we are known as "Shirdhonkar."

Our ancestors moved from Maharashtra to Gwalior about 250 years ago, during the time of Mahadji Scindia. They were recognized as *Shiledars* (cavalry officers) of the Scindia Royal Family.

Hindus have a family deity known as *Kuladevata*, which each family is expected to worship with utmost faith and devotion across generations. Both the Scindia royal family and the Shirdhonkar family share the same *Kuladevata*, known as Jyotiba Kedar. The temple of Jyotiba Kedar is located approximately 12 kilometers from Kolhapur, on the way to Wadi in Ratnagiri Tehsil, at a place known as Jyotiba Dongar.

It is said that Jyotiba is an incarnation of Lord Shiva, whom the local people implored to descend to Wadi Ratnagiri to eliminate *Asuras*—anti-social elements that had emerged in large numbers in the region. Among these, Ratnasoor was the principal evil spirit, whose reign of terror had caused immense fear and anxiety among peace-loving people.

In response to their pleas, Lord Shiva came in the form of Jyotiba Kedar. However, concern arose among the divine beings that Ratnasoor might harm Lord Shiva, as he was blessed with immortality. To aid him, Goddess Chopdai and Goddess Yamuna Devi brought a jar of nectar and joined forces with Lord Shiva in his battle against Ratnasoor. After a prolonged and fierce fight, Lord Shiva, with the support of these divine beings, finally vanquished Ratnasoor.

This story symbolizes the victory of truth and peace over evil, underscoring the divine commitment to the welfare of humanity.

My First Ever Memory

My first memory dates back to an incident in Shamshabad, a small town in Vidisha District (formerly part of the Gwalior state), where my father received his first appointment as a Sub-Inspector of Police. Strangely, I have no recollection of any specific interactions with my parents or others during our time in Shamshabad.

One vivid memory, however, stands out: perhaps unknowingly, I wandered away from the house without my parents' knowledge, ran onto the street, and found myself mesmerized by the sunrise at the edge of a bridge. I can still recall enjoying the moment for about ten minutes before someone brought me back home.

Beyond this brief but profound memory, no other recollection of Shamshabad has stayed with me to this day. I must have been barely three years old at the time. It seems that memories from such an early stage of life often fade away with the passage of time, leaving behind only a few fleeting impressions.

My Father's Posting in Tonk Khurd

My father was later transferred to Tonk-Khurd in Ujjain District (now part of Dewas District). Tonk was a tribal region predominantly inhabited by the Kunjar tribal community. Looting travelers on the rural *kachcha* roads was a common occurrence and, unfortunately, a customary occupation for many in this community. The police often had to arrest them, sometimes in groups, and temporarily detain them under the open sky for a night. Subsequently, they were sent to Ujjain for trial and further legal proceedings.

We lived in a spacious police station building, with our residential quarters on the first floor and the police station occupying the ground floor. In front of the building lay a vast open field, and across from it stood a primary school. We owned a horse and a cow, and every morning, my elder brother and I would drink fresh cow's milk. Tea was not an option for us for many years, as milk remained a staple part of our mornings.

Maharashtrians in MP

I still remember that there were two or three Marathi-speaking families in the area, but we were better acquainted with the Kasture family. Their son was around our age, and we spent most of our time together, either playing games or learning from one another. After a few months, we moved to Ujjain as my father was transferred to another police station in Jahangirpur, near Nagda. In Ujjain, we stayed for a few months with the Panse family in the Malipura area, near Dewas Gate.

***

Chapter 2

Loss of Eyesight

"Sometimes life doesn't give you something you want, not because you don't deserve it, but because you deserve something BETTER."

-Anonymous

We lost our mother when I was about five years old, leaving behind only faint impressions of her in my memory. It was around 1936 or 1937 when we were deprived of a mother's care and affection. After her passing, our father and grandmother took on the responsibility of raising us.

I inherited blindness in my left eye, and it was believed that my mother had watched a solar eclipse with the naked eye while pregnant with me. At that time, this was considered a myth, even in the medical community. However, in the 21st century, medical science has supported the idea that viewing a solar eclipse can potentially affect a child's eyes in the womb, which is why pregnant women are now advised to avoid looking at the eclipse.

Hence initially, I was not admitted to any school. My father feared that the strain of reading and writing might harm the limited vision in my only functional eye. However, my curiosity and determination led me to sit in a classroom on my own, for several days without formal admission. Eventually, the teacher insisted that my father fill out the admission form. Reluctantly, he agreed, and I was finally allowed to begin regular schooling—a decision shaped more by my persistence than his approval.

Up until the 3rd standard, I studied at Ujjain, after which I continued my education in Gwalior. There was an interruption of about a year in my schooling due to family circumstances and my grandfather's hesitation in taking on the responsibility for our education.

Despite these challenges, I completed my primary and upper-primary education with vision in only one eye. Throughout those years, my peers regarded me as an intelligent student and often saw me as an ideal student in the class. The education I received during that time played a significant role in helping me manage both my academic progress and rehabilitation in the years to come. Even back then, English was taught using Basic English Primer books, and it was a compulsory subject from the first standard. Additionally, vocational education was a key component of the upper primary classes.

However, in 1946, I lost that remaining vision. My father took me to Gwalior and had me examined by an experienced ophthalmologist. I was very happy and hopeful about my treatment. However, in the same year, during September, my father underwent surgery for a hernia and could not recover. He left us for his heavenly abode. I was just 14 years old. Nature deprived us of our father too, who was the only support for my brother and me.

From that point onward, we faced life like orphans. It was indeed a tough phase for us. We were in turmoil and found no one around, to offer a helping hand! Teenage, which is supposed to be full of dreams, hope, and enthusiasm, was suddenly disrupted. We had to survive at the mercy of nature and rely on those closer relatives who may or may not be committed to helping us move ahead.

During that phase, I happened to listen to the personal interview of veteran film actor Shashikala, conducted by Mr. Unees Khan on the radio program “Sitaren.” I noticed that her childhood was, to some extent, similar to mine. The journey from starvation to satisfaction or lasting peace mirrored our experiences. Like her, I lost my mother in early childhood, and my elder brother and I were raised by our father. There were many days when we had to sleep without dinner, sometimes with just a glass of water or some Sev Parmal (snacks) to sustain us. At the age of thirteen, Shashikala received Rs. 20/- as her first income, for which she expressed gratitude to the Almighty and celebrated it as we celebrate the Diwali festival. Similarly, I had a few occasions when I earned small amounts by selling daily utility items, house to house, in the surrounding vicinity.

***

Chapter 3

The Aftermath

"There is always the battle to be fought before the victory is won."

-Dean Stanley

We faced severe hardships almost every day, struggling to make ends meet. There were occasions when we could only manage one meal a day and had to skip dinner. Even my elder brother, Mr. Dattatraya, delivered newspapers door-to-door to support his educational needs; it was our only source of sustenance.

The evil eye of family members and society was felt deeply during those three years. I was almost entirely disassociated from my family solely because of my blindness.

I still feel agony when I recall an incident where my relatives took my elderly grandfather from Gwalior to Mandsaur for cataract surgery at a government hospital where a renowned eye surgeon worked. However, at that time, no one showed any concern to take me along for treatment! Despite my efforts to convince them, it was in vain. I was deprived of the opportunity to be examined by an ophthalmologist. Timely intervention might have preserved my residual vision and significantly aided my education and rehabilitation in the years to come.

Another incident that deeply shakes my emotions occurred when all the family members went to Ratlam to attend a marriage, leaving me ALONE for THREE DAYS in Ujjain! Can you imagine that? They merely advised one of our tenants to look after me, that too for formality. I was neither too old to manage entirely on my own nor too young to ignore the indifferent and negative attitude of the family.

These two incidents alone lay bare the harsh truth: If family members themselves can be the so cruel and uncaring toward a blind person within their own blood, what care to expect from the general public, who are not even related to me?!

Between September 1946 and July 1949, a period of about three years, we lost our aunt, eldest uncle, and then our grandfather. This loss disrupted the lives of three families—those of the three brothers. If the family felt 'disrupted,' you can imagine how I, being blind and helpless, must have felt. It was a time of panic, a period of exile for me. Isolation, starvation, and the indifferent attitude of others forced me to face a dreadful, nearly fatal existence. Though these events belong to the distant past, even today, I struggle to express the agonies, stress, and strain I endured due to the inhuman treatment I received during those days.

There were moments when I contemplated ending my life. However, the inner strength I was blessed with helped me find the courage to face the adversity and wait for a positive change. Deep in my heart, there was always hope that life would eventually guide me to a better destination. The inner core of my heart truly felt the agony of a blind child deprived of parents. This realization inspired me to extend care and support to children facing similar adversity of being left with inhuman relatives, in the absence of loving parents.

***

Chapter 4

V M School for the Blind – My Cradle of Rebirth

"Being ignorant is not as much a shame as being unwilling to learn."

- Benjamin Franklin

It is said that a person dies many times in their life. Adversities of various kinds drain courage, erode confidence, and bring a person to the brink of despair. For example, a child deprived of their parents in early life, a newlywed couple who faces an accident in which the husband dies, leaving the wife to confront the world alone—these are the complex calamities one must face in life. Many of us often face such incidents, and I was no exception. However, the conditions I faced were even more critical and complex, as I was dealing with physical disabilities and social neglect. There seemed to be no escape from such a dire existence.

Yet, in these moments of crisis, one must gather their inner strength with patience and reorganize themselves to emerge completely transformed. This transformed being is known as *Dwija*—twice-born, a rebirth of spirit and resilience.

In 1949, a man named Mr. Kulkarni from Mumbai moved to Ujjain and, by chance, decided to stay in our house near the Mahakal Temple. He had retired from the railways and wanted to settle in Ujjain. A sensitive soul, he took the time to understand my condition and, knowing my deep desire for an education, advised me to join a school for the blind, either in Mumbai or elsewhere. Eager for such an opportunity, I asked him to help me get admission to a school in Mumbai. Without hesitation, he wrote to a friend and secured an admission form from the Victoria Memorial School for the Blind, located on Tardeo Road, Mumbai. Within a couple of days, the form arrived, and my uncle filled it out and sent it back to the institution.

I waited anxiously, filled with hope, and in June, we received a letter of consent from the Principal for my admission. It was a turning point that transformed my entire life, and I often refer to it as “A Moment of Rebirth.” This moment became the light that guided me forward, boosting my morale and giving me the strength to face the challenges that lay ahead.

On Thursday, July 7, 1949, I stepped into the institution, marking a golden day in my life as I entered the temple of hope and solace.

The Principal, Mr. K. N. K. Jussaawala, was a man of remarkable character, with a deep sensitivity toward addressing the educational needs of blind children. The school offered academic education only up to the seventh standard, which I had already completed while studying alongside sighted children in a regular school. As a result, my status in the school was recognized at a different level.

The establishment of Victoria Memorial School for the Blind was closely linked to the inspiring story of Dr. Neelkanthrai

Chhatrapaty from Gujarat. He lost his eyesight suddenly and, in search of better treatment, was taken to the UK. Unfortunately, he could not regain his vision. However, this life-altering experience gave him a new perspective—a "vision through blindness." Motivated by this experience, he resolved to address the urgent need for educating children who had lost their sight.

In 1901, following the passing of Queen Victoria, a trust was formed to establish a hospital in her memory. However, Dr. Neelkanthrai Chhatrapaty, driven by his vision for the education of blind children, traveled to the UK and persuaded the trustees to re-purpose the project into a school for the blind instead of a hospital. The trustees agreed, and the building initially intended for an eye hospital became the Victoria Memorial School for the Blind. Through his efforts, Dr. Chhatrapaty opened the doors to knowledge and dignity for blind children who might otherwise have remained in perpetual darkness.

I was instructed to learn Braille, music, chair caning, and other skills. I attended classes in all these areas, but I didn't find the instruction engaging or enjoyable. However, I developed a keen interest in learning English Braille. Within six months, I was able to read and write English Braille at a level that allowed me to access books in the library. Perhaps I was the only student truly utilizing the library's resources.

At that time, there was no uniformity in the Braille system used for Indian languages. It was impossible for a blind student from one institution to read Braille books from another, as different schools employed different systems. In 1952, the centennial death anniversary of Louis Braille was commemorated worldwide, and UNESCO played a crucial role in advocating for the standardization of Braille. A conference was held in Beirut to devise strategies for achieving Braille uniformity. Shri. Lal Advani, Special Officer of the Department of Education, Government of

India, attended along with Shri. Rustamji Alpaiwala, then president of the National Association for the Blind (NAB). As a result, the Bharti Braille system was introduced for all Indian languages. This made it possible to transcribe books into Braille in various Indian languages across the country.

Due to my active participation in various extracurricular activities, I was elected Secretary of the Student Committee. Later, I was selected as a member of the Executive Council of the Blind Men's Association. In 1952, I had the privilege of witnessing the founding of the National Association for the Blind, which played a significant role in promoting comprehensive services for the blind at the national level.

During this time, I learned that Mr. Rajendra T. Vyas and Mr. Devdhar, both blind students, were pursuing college education. This inspired me to pursue higher education as well. Additionally, Mr. Suresh Ahuja, another blind youth, had completed his Master's degree at the London School of Economics. These three blind individuals became national role models, proving that a university education was attainable for the blind in our country.

Thus, this was truly a moment of dawn in my life. Through the blessings of the Almighty, I gained the perspective and determination to move forward, enabling me to continue my education and life despite the overwhelming challenges.

***

Chapter 5

Professional Education: Physiotherapy

"Learning is not attained by chance, it must be sought for with ardor and attended to with diligence."

-Abigail Adams

Significant Developments

The year 1952 was a significant year for the cause of the blind, both in India and around the world. It marked a grand tribute to Louis Braille, the inventor of the Braille script. His remains were moved from his family grave to the National Cemetery in Paris. This was done 100 years after his death to honor his remarkable contribution to the education of the blind. Dr. Helen Keller, along with many educators and other dignitaries, walked 40 kilometers from Coupvray to Paris to pay their respects to this great man.

In the same year, the National Association for the Blind was established in India. This organization became a key player in promoting services for the blind and later set up branches in various states and districts. The efforts in 1952 gave a strong push to the cause of the blind, bringing about significant progress at both state and national levels.

Shri. K. N. K. Jussawala, Principal of Victoria School for the Blind, went to the UK for six months of training in blind education. The year 1952 also marked the Golden Jubilee of the school. On this special occasion, Pt. Jawaharlal Nehru, the then Prime Minister of India, visited the institution along with his daughter, Mrs. Indira Gandhi.

It is worth mentioning that the Prime Minister graciously accepted the students' heartfelt request to attend the celebration. The excitement among us was unmatched as we prepared to welcome him with a 'Guard of Honor.' For me, it was a moment of great pride to personally present a self-made bag to Pt. Nehru, lovingly known as 'Chacha Nehru,' on this memorable day.

Choosing Physiotherapy

After schooling at V M School for the Blind, I had to choose a suitable career oath for myself. After wanted a career path that would not only provide economic independence but also allow me to serve those in need. Hence I began considering Physiotherapy. Coincidently V M School for the Blind offered professional training in physiotherapy! Thus, I wholeheartedly embraced this opportunity and enrolled for the three-year program with genuine interest and dedication.

Hostel Problem

The institution's rules prohibited me from using the hostel facilities which I had been using during my schooling all this while. This created a serious challenge to the completion of my physiotherapy training. During this time, Shri. R. Alpaiwala was serving as the officiating principal in Mr. K N K Jussawala's absence, as he was on an educational tour. I confided in Mr. Alpaiwala about my difficulties in finding accommodation outside the institution. He kindly intervened and arranged for me to stay at the NSD Home for the Blind, located at Worli, for my lodging and boarding needs.

My early education was in Marathi, my mother tongue, and I had minimal exposure to Hindi before I lost my eyesight. However, with Hindi being declared the national language, efforts to promote its learning intensified, particularly through organizations like the Rashtra Bhasha Prachar Samiti, Wardha. During my stay at the NSD Home, I seized the opportunity to improve my proficiency and successfully appeared for the Praveshika Examination conducted by the Samiti. This marked an important step in broadening my linguistic skills and adapting to the evolving educational landscape.

Though NSD Home had offered me place to stay, its environment was not conducive to my well-being, and I could only endure the conditions for about four months. As per the rules, only trainees were allowed to stay there, and I was unable to undertake any vocational training offered at the Home, which added to my struggles. Faced with these regulations, I sought help from a friend and moved to a place near the GPO in Fort, though it was also not an ideal living situation.

In April 1954, I met with Mr. Jussawala and shared my distressing experiences with him—how I was struggling with mobility challenges and financial constraints while staying outside the institution. It seemed like my only option was to leave my training early and return to Ujjain. But somehow, the Almighty had other plans for me.

Principal Mr. Jussawala shared some wonderful news with me. He read aloud a letter from the Ministry of Education, Government of India, informing me that I had been awarded a scholarship of Rs. 100 per month for the upcoming academic year. This news filled me with immense joy and relief. With the scholarship secured, I decided to look for a better hostel.

I found one hostel named 'Pathak Lodge', which was located in Devkaran Mansion on Princess Street, Mumbai. Devkaran Mansion was a large building with streets on all four sides, very close to Crawford Market. My friend and classmate, Mr. Chandrakant Doshi, was also staying in the same building, just on the opposite side. The building housed a hostel exclusively for male youths from the Shwetamber Jain Community. The residents of the hostel were mostly involved in self-employment ventures, and their stay there was typically short-term, usually lasting one to two years.

Mr. Chandrakant Doshi managed to arrange a hostel for me at Pathak Lodge. We then attended physiotherapy classes together and returned home daily throughout the rest of the academic session.

Marine Drive Exhibition Stall

Mr. C. K. Doshi and I used to travel together to school and other places. On one occasion, we both managed a stall at a large exhibition organized at the Marine Drive seafront during the centennial celebration of the textile industry in India. The stall was sponsored by Victoria Memorial School for the Blind, and the principal asked us to run it on their behalf.

However, we faced a major challenge—there was no funding available to manage the stall for such a prestigious national exhibition. Our determination, though, was unyielding. Despite the lack of resources, we managed to contribute only Rs.12 each as a small capital to purchase certain cutlery and hosiery items. We also negotiated to take some items on a one-week credit. Despite the limited funds, we set up the stall and attended it every evening from 6 PM to 11 PM, working for a month on two separate occasions.

What amazed both the customers and us was that a blind person could independently run such a stall. Remarkably, not a single item from our counter was stolen. In fact, many customers were so impressed by the initiative that they bought products just to encourage our efforts. By the end of the two exhibitions, we had saved Rs.1000 and two tins of chocolate—an incredible return on our initial investment of only Rs.24 in total.

This experience filled us with encouragement and confidence, making us even more determined to undertake similar ventures in the future. It was a testament to how sheer determination and teamwork can overcome challenges and lead to success.

Interesting Friends

Almost a year later in Pathak Lodge, an elderly Gujarati-speaking man came to stay in my room, right in front of my cot. He was living alone, as his son-in-law and daughter were unable to accommodate him in their home. So, they arranged for his stay at Pathak Lodge. It was during my conversations with him that I first began to realize the socio-economic challenges faced by older people and the conditions they often have to endure.

The old man had plenty of time to read books, which he would get from a local library. One day, he brought a handbook titled 'Thus Spake Vivekananda', which he read to me every day. The teachings in that book were incredibly inspiring for leading a positive life. Most of the content was directed at young Indians, urging them to contribute to the nation-building of a "New India."

The impact of these thoughts on me was profound, and they helped shape my positive attitude toward life, society, and the nation. Even now, I have kept a copy of that handbook, which serves as a reminder of my time at Pathak Lodge. Two quotations from the book that left a lasting impression on me are:

"All power is within you; you can do anything and everything. Believe in that; do not believe that you are weak; do not believe that you are half-crazy lunatics. You can do anything and everything without even the guidance of anyone. All power is there. Stand up and express the divinity within you."

"I am superior to many; I am inferior to a few, but nowhere am I the last, and I can also do something."

One of my friends, Mr. Baburao Kadam, was a teacher at the nearby Happy Home and School for the Blind. He taught craft, but he also had remarkable skills as a palmist. He lived in a shared room within the school building, and after school hours, a steady stream of clients would come to him for palm readings. From 3 PM until 8 PM, he was busy with clients, who had great faith in his predictions. His forecasts were not only accurate but also deeply resonated with his clients, making him highly regarded for his ability to foresee the future.

Then there was Mr. Chowdhary, who worked as a tailoring teacher. It was the first time I observed how a blind person could manage the intricate task of cutting cloth for shirts, pajamas, and other garments! He explained that tailoring was a family tradition, and it was through this background that he developed the skills necessary for the craft. His ability to navigate the sewing machine and fabric with such precision was truly inspiring, showing me that even in the face of blindness, one could master a skill and make a living.

Then, I came across Shri. Govind Ahuja, a refugee who was blind, and who kept himself occupied with transcription work, particularly transcribing the Bhagavad Gita into Braille. The transcription project was sponsored by a trust, and the Braille copies of the Gita were distributed free of charge to interested blind individuals. For Shri. Ahuja, this transcription work was his primary source of income, and it made me realize the potential of

Braille transcription as an income-generating activity for Braille writers. It was a remarkable example of how a skill could not only support one's livelihood but also serve a greater cause.

During this time, I came to know about another blind friend, Mr. Ratnakar Raje, who was successfully studying in a regular secondary school. This pioneering example was truly inspiring and sparked a deep motivation within me to continue my education as a lifelong pursuit, even after completing my physiotherapy training. His determination reinforced my belief that, with the right mindset and effort, no goal was beyond reach.

Extracurricular Activities

Alongside my training in Physiotherapy, I actively participated in a variety of sports events and won prizes in different competitions. It was a fantastic opportunity to engage in physical activities and develop a sense of teamwork and resilience.

One particularly memorable experience was meeting Shri. Vijay Merchant, then captain of the Indian cricket team and an esteemed philanthropist. His visit to the school was an inspiring moment for all of us, and it helped to motivate me and my peers to pursue our own goals and dreams with greater vigor.

Additionally, I had the privilege of enrolling in the Scout movement and playing the role of Troop Leader in various related activities. On December 6, 1952, under my troop's leadership, we were honored to provide a guard of honor to the Honorable Prime Minister, Pandit Jawaharlal Nehru. It was an unforgettable experience that underscored the importance of discipline, respect, and civic duty.

Seeing my achievements, I was then elected as Secretary of the Student Committee, I was entrusted with numerous responsibilities, one of which was managing conflicts among the students. Frequently, disagreements would arise over various issues, and it became my role to act as a counselor, helping students resolve their differences and encouraging them to treat each other with respect and dignity.

A recurring issue revolved around the school's radio programs. At the time, the school had only one radio, and we had a group of 50 students, divided equally between Marathi and Gujarati speakers. The problem arose when popular radio programs, particularly dramas, were broadcast in both languages at the same time. This created a conflict, as neither group could listen to their preferred program simultaneously.

The situation escalated when students from both groups complained to Principal Mr. Jussawala. He calmly listened to the concerns of both sides and then called me to find a solution. After a few meetings with both groups, I suggested that we alternate between Marathi and Gujarati dramas on different days. This would allow each group to enjoy their preferred programs without conflict. Both groups agreed to this arrangement, and it worked to everyone's satisfaction. Additionally, I encouraged the students to listen to some Hindi programs as well, helping them improve their Hindi language skills in the process.

This experience was not only a lesson in conflict resolution but also in fostering a sense of compromise and cooperation among diverse groups.

Influencing Personalities

My Physiotherapy training at Victoria Memorial School for the Blind played a significant role in shaping my personality. The influence of certain individuals left a lasting impact on me:

Meeting Dr. Hellen Keller!

Dr. Helen Keller visited India, and we had the incredible privilege of welcoming her to our institution. Accompanied by her interpreter, Ms. Polly Thompson, she entered our classroom and personally shook hands with each of us. It was a moment of unparalleled joy and honor, one that has stayed with me as a cherished memory to this day. The happiness and excitement I felt were beyond words. It was as if every part of me was alive with energy, an inner echo of disbelief and delight. I remember pinching myself three times just to confirm that I wasn't dreaming. Meeting my idol, Helen Keller, felt like a dream turned into reality. Even now, the memory remains vivid and fresh, as though it happened just this morning—a truly unforgettable experience.

Mr. Jussawala

Mr. K. N. K. Jussawala, the Principal of our school had a profound effect on my growth, guiding me to regulate my behavior, focus on social responsibility, and cultivate self-respect and human dignity.

Mrs. Rani Khetwala

The Matron of the school, Mrs. Rani Khetwala, was another person who played a pivotal role in our lives. She cared for all the students with a motherly affection, and we all called her "Mamma." She was responsible for our health and well-being, looking after our day-to-day needs. In her spare time, she also taught knitting to selected students, and I was fortunate to benefit from her teachings for a few days. Additionally, I learned typing with the help of her daughter, Ms. Gullu, who was about my age. Learning English typing proved to be a valuable skill, as it helped me overcome the barriers of written communication with sighted people.

Mr. Alpaiwala

While working as the officiating Principal of the school, Mr. Alpaiwala used a regular typewriter for his record-keeping. It was from him that I got inspired to learn typing. Mr. and Mrs. Alpaiwala were active members of Theosophical Society of India, and Mrs. Alpaiwala would often read materials on various religions. She emphasized the importance of developing a strength in the integrated approach to understanding all religions. This teaching had a significant impact on me, highlighting the value of harmony and unity across different faiths.

Dr. Jogas

Lastly, Dr. Jogas, our physiotherapist instructor, dedicated three years to training us in physiotherapy with great commitment. Along with my fellow students, I benefited immensely from his teachings, gaining the confidence that the profession of physiotherapy could provide a viable career for our livelihood. His guidance helped shape our futures, making it possible for us to serve others while sustaining ourselves through this meaningful profession.

Passing with Flying Colors!

Several physicians from medical colleges and practicing doctors came to our school and taught us different subjects. I was also fortunate to receive Braille textbooks from RNIB London, which significantly helped me strengthen my understanding at this advanced level.

Thus, with having such a rich experience in education, in April 1955, I successfully cleared my examinations in Physiotherapy on the first attempt, securing the 1st Rank among 10 students!

***

Chapter 6

My Physiotherapy Practice

"Determine to like your work. Then it will become a pleasure, not drudgery. Perhaps you do not need to change your job. Change yourself and your work will seem different."

- Dr. Norman Vincent Peale

My Private Clinic

Having cleared my Physiotherapy examination, in April 1955, I left Mumbai, carrying with me the sweet memories of my time at Victoria Memorial School for the Blind. My departure was bittersweet, as I had formed deep associations with my peers, teachers, and dignitaries who had been instrumental in shaping my journey. As I stepped out, I felt a heavy weight in my heart, a sense of being alone to face the harsh realities of life. I had neither financial security nor emotional support to rely on.

My journey first took me to Ujjain, and from there, I visited Gwalior for a few days. At that point, I found myself at a crossroads, with two career paths ahead of me. The first option was to join Madhav Blind School in Gwalior as the in-charge of the institution, a role that offered stability and responsibility. The second was to establish myself in Indore as a practicing physiotherapist. Indore, with its numerous medical practitioners, held the potential for referrals and a steady stream of patients in need of physiotherapy. After careful thought, I decided to take the road less traveled and establish my practice in Indore, depending purely on referrals from doctors.

It was a challenging yet hopeful decision, driven by my belief in physiotherapy as a viable career and my aspiration to make a meaningful contribution to society. This decision marked the beginning of a new chapter in my life, one filled with opportunities to grow both professionally and personally.

Upon arriving in Indore, I found myself striving to establish a foothold in an unfamiliar environment. During this time, I was fortunate to meet Dr. J. N. Pohawala, a professor of pediatric medicine, and Dr. Chamanlal Nagrath, a lecturer in orthopedics at MGM Medical College. Their cordial demeanor and assurances of patient referrals for physiotherapy offered me a glimmer of hope as I ventured into professional practice.

For the initial few months, I stayed with my maternal uncle, whose family extended immense kindness and provided lodging and boarding during this transitional phase. Despite their support, the uncertainty of my future weighed heavily on my mind. For a fortnight, I eagerly awaited the promised patient referrals from Dr. Pohawala and Dr. Nagrath. The delay in receiving cases left me anxious about the viability of continuing in Indore.

Finally, one evening, Dr. Pohawala referred my first patient—a two-year-old child suffering from poliomyelitis. The child required physiotherapy to regain muscle strength and improve mobility. With diligent treatment sessions conducted at the child's residence, I worked consistently for two months. Slowly but steadily, the child showed remarkable improvement, eventually standing and taking a few steps with support. Witnessing the joy and gratitude of the child's parents brought an immense sense of fulfillment and confidence to me.

This breakthrough marked the beginning of my physiotherapy practice in Indore. The momentum gained from this initial success not only solidified my resolve to stay but also paved the way for a promising career in helping others regain their mobility and independence.

Determined to secure my future and serve the community, I made the decision to establish a physiotherapy clinic in Indore. This marked a significant milestone in my journey. On August 15, 1955, a day of great national pride, my clinic was inaugurated by the esteemed High Court Justice Shri. Newaskar, making it a truly memorable occasion. This event held special significance as it marked the opening of the very first physiotherapy clinic in Madhya Pradesh, and I became recognized as the first physiotherapist in the state.

The clinic quickly gained attention, attracting patients who had been seeking relief from various ailments through other means without success. The effectiveness of physiotherapy as a treatment method began to resonate with the public. Within just a few months, my practice grew to accommodate 6-8 patients daily—a number sufficient for me to sustain myself while establishing a reputation in the field. This initial success not only validated my decision but also set the foundation for a rewarding career dedicated to improving the lives of others through physiotherapy.

M. Y. Government Hospital, Indore

Building professional relationships with the medical community required persistent effort. Gradually, through hard work and consistent results, I earned their trust and referrals. However, I realized early on that private practice in physiotherapy alone might not yield a stable income. Recognizing this, I decided to explore opportunities within the government sector to secure a more sustainable future.

The post of physiotherapist at M. Y. Government Hospital, Indore, which was affiliated with MGM Medical College, presented itself as a promising opportunity. Pursuing this position was far from easy, though. Convincing senior government officials and medical authorities of my competence and professional capabilities was an uphill battle. It required not just demonstrating my skills but also breaking down preconceived notions about the limitations of a blind therapist. Despite these challenges, my determination to prove my worth remained steadfast.

Determined to secure the post of Physiotherapist in a government hospital, I embraced the adage, *“Where there is a will, there is a way.”* With unwavering resolve, I pursued my case, even as the newly reorganized Madhya Pradesh emerged in November 1956, uniting Mahakaushal, Madhyabharat, and Bhopal into one state. The advent of this new state brought new challenges, but also new opportunities.

In January 1957, during the first visit of Mr. H. V. Pataskar, the inaugural Governor of Madhya Pradesh and a former Central Law Minister, I seized the chance to present my case to him personally. I explained my qualifications and emphasized the importance of creating opportunities for individuals like me within the state itself. Initially, the Governor saw the matter as a daunting challenge, advising me to consider moving back to Bombay, where blind physiotherapists had already secured exceptional positions in government hospitals.

However, I humbly but firmly expressed the injustice of such advice. I argued that it was unreasonable to expect skilled professionals to leave their home state for employment when the new Madhya Pradesh should instead strive to provide equal opportunities to all its residents. Highlighting the state’s oversight of the “right to work,” I appealed to his sense of fairness and justice.

Moved by my arguments and the reality of the situation, the Governor assured me that he would personally recommend my case to the government for due consideration. His words rekindled my hope, and I felt a renewed sense of purpose as I awaited the outcome of his intervention.

Fueled by hope and determination after my meeting with the Governor, I decided to take matters further and headed to Bhopal, the state capital. Accompanied by my 13-year-old cousin, Eknath, who acted as my guide and constant companion, I navigated the city in pursuit of the decision-makers who could help my case.

One morning, I managed to secure an audience with Mrs. Padmavati Raje, the Minister for Health. She listened attentively to my story and assured me of her support, promising to take the necessary action on my behalf. Encouraged by her words, I felt a renewed sense of optimism.

The next day, I took my efforts to the State Legislative Assembly, where a session was underway. With the assistance of two Members of the Legislative Assembly (MLAs) from Indore, I arranged a meeting with the Chief Minister, Shri. Kailash Nath Katju. A statesman of great intellect, he immediately recognized the potential of my rare skills and the importance of utilizing them for the public good. He understood that my work as a physiotherapist could greatly benefit the community through government services.

In a gesture that felt like a breakthrough, the Chief Minister personally wrote a letter addressed to the officer in charge at the Directorate of Health Services in Indore, recommending my case. Holding that letter in my hands, I returned to Indore with a heart brimming with hope and anticipation, confident that my efforts were finally about to bear fruit.

The next morning in Indore, faced with severe financial hardship, I set out with my Bhabhiji (sister-in-law) to meet Dr. S. K. Kaul, the Deputy Director of Health Services. With the

Chief Minister's letter in hand, we walked over 8 kilometers to his bungalow, unable to afford public transport. Each step was a testament to the struggle and hope that had brought me this far.

When we reached, I handed Dr. Kaul the letter and explained my plight. I painted a picture of the dire circumstances we were enduring: my elder brother, newly married just two years prior, was suffering from schizophrenia, a debilitating mental illness that had forced him to leave his job in Jodhpur. With three of us unemployed and no alternative source of income, the weight of survival bore heavily on us.

Dr. Kaul listened attentively and showed an unexpected kindness. He assured us that my sister-in-law would be given an office job and asked her to visit him at his office the next day. Regarding my case, he was forthright, explaining that government processes might take some time but assured me that my request was being considered seriously.

Though my case was not resolved immediately, Dr. Kaul's gesture of extending a job opportunity to my Bhabhiji felt like a lifeline amidst the storm. It gave us a glimmer of hope, a small step towards stability in an otherwise uncertain future.

In the third week of November 1957, much to my surprise and relief, I received the long-awaited appointment order for the post of Physiotherapist at MY Hospital, Indore. It marked a significant turning point in my journey. The initial appointment was for six months, on a provisional basis, with the stipulation that I would need to appear before the Public Service Commission for selection and confirmation.

After one year, I appeared before the Public Service Commission (PSC) for the formal selection process. Despite having demonstrated my capabilities during the year, I faced competition from sighted physiotherapists. Although I had proven my expertise, I was unable to meet their specific qualification requirements and, as a result, was not selected by the PSC. My services were terminated in December 1958.

During that year, I had the opportunity to treat the Chairman of the Public Service Commission at the hospital, and he was highly satisfied with my physiotherapy services. Reliable sources later informed me that in his report to the government, the Chairman expressed his support for me, recommending that the government create another position so my services could continue to benefit the public. He emphasized that this would not only serve the community but also help raise awareness of the potential that individuals, regardless of blindness, can offer.

As a result, the government decided to appoint me as a Junior Physiotherapist, officially designated as Masseur. I did not have to exert much effort to secure this position and joined the hospital on 25 April 1959. I continued to serve in this role until the end of December 1991, marking the longest and most fulfilling chapter of my professional journey as a Physiotherapist!

Curing Patients

In the early years, from 1957 to 1959, consultants were curious about the therapeutic effects of physiotherapy. As a result, several chronic cases were referred to me to assess my abilities and demonstrate the potential benefits of physiotherapy. One such case involved a patient who had suffered from persistent back pain for 12 years.

Upon investigation, I discovered that the patient was a goldsmith by trade, having been engaged in this occupation since childhood. His work required him to sit for long hours in a fixed posture, which led to the back pain. Identifying the root cause of the issue, I prescribed a series of specific back exercises, followed by a hot tub bath.

The treatment proved effective, and the patient found relief from the pain. Gradually, he was able to return to his normal routine, free from the debilitating backache that had troubled him for years. This case further reinforced the value of physiotherapy in treating chronic conditions and solidified my confidence in this healing profession.

Another patient, a 30-year-old Food Inspector, was referred to me with severe arthritis. He was bedridden due to contractures in his hips, knees, ankles, wrists, and fingers. For nearly three months, I treated him with a targeted physiotherapy regimen. Through consistent therapy, most of the contractures were successfully released, and the patient regained enough strength to stand and walk with some support. Eventually, he was able to ride a bicycle to his office, a remarkable recovery given his condition.

The consultants were astounded by the progress and the seemingly miraculous results. Their initial skepticism was replaced with strong belief in the effectiveness of physiotherapy. These cases not only solidified my reputation as a competent physiotherapist but also demonstrated the crucial role of physiotherapy in medical rehabilitation, earning the trust and confidence of the medical community.

A Fulfilling Career Afterall!

Choosing physiotherapy as my profession turned out to be one of the most fulfilling decisions of my life. From 1955 to 1991, I dedicated myself to this field, witnessing its transformative impact on patients and gaining immense satisfaction from helping them regain functionality and independence. At the time I started, physiotherapy was relatively unknown, and public awareness of its potential was minimal. However, it soon proved its effectiveness in addressing numerous crippling conditions.

Physiotherapy became a cornerstone of physical rehabilitation, especially for neurological and orthopedic disorders. Common neurological conditions such as hemiplegia, monoplegia, paraplegia, and Bell's palsy were treated with significant success. One of the most prevalent conditions during my early years was poliomyelitis, which affected countless children. Physiotherapy proved instrumental in their recovery, helping them regain mobility and lead fuller lives.

Orthopedic cases, particularly those resulting from accidents and multiple fractures, were another area where physiotherapy excelled. The treatment focused on restoring joint mobility and muscle power, crucial for patients' recovery. Chronic conditions like rheumatoid arthritis and deformities requiring orthosis were also managed effectively through physiotherapy.

In many instances, physiotherapy achieved results that surpassed those of medicines or alternative treatments, demonstrating its vital role in patient care. The ability to restore hope and functionality in patients made every moment of my career deeply rewarding.

Introducing physiotherapy to Indore in Madhya Pradesh was a significant milestone—not just for the city but also for me as a blind therapist. The novelty of a visually impaired professional excelling in such a technical field sparked both surprise and curiosity among the general public and medical professionals alike.

I was pleasantly surprised and deeply honored when Mr. R. Bhattacharya, the hospital superintendent, offered to issue a reference certificate stating, *"Even though Mr. M. V. Shirdhonkar is a visually impaired person, he is excellent in his profession and earns the appreciable confidence of his patients."* Similarly, another surgeon, Mr. S. Kumar, described me in his reference letter as *"Mr. M. V. Shirdhonkar is an asset to the profession of physiotherapy and the institution concerned."* These words of recognition brought immense joy and motivation to continue striving in my work.

My employment as a physiotherapist at the government hospital paved the way for a new career opportunity for the visually impaired in Madhya Pradesh. I sincerely hope and expect that other dedicated visually impaired individuals in the state will also consider joining this noble profession.

***

Chapter 7

MP Welfare Association for the Blind

"The purpose of human life is to serve, and to show compassion and the will to help others."

-Albert Schweitzer

The Seed

While striving for a government job, the challenges I faced—much like the earlier struggles during my training period in Mumbai—often compelled me to reflect on the broader hardships of the visually impaired community. It became a deeply ingrained conviction in my heart that no visually challenged individual, especially young people, should have to endure such intense struggles for education, employment, or social well-being.

Shri. M. M. Thorat, Principal and Secretary of the Deaf Dumb Blind School, was instrumental in helping me establish myself in Indore for employment and initiating services for the blind. His colleague, Shri. J. M. Bhagat, also contributed significantly, serving as Honorary Secretary during the initial years of the organization.

It was evident that a robust voluntary organization was needed, one led by well-trained professionals, ideally including a visually impaired individual with firsthand experience. Additionally, the organization required the active participation of enlightened and committed citizens dedicated to serving the cause of the visually impaired.

In May 1959, I took the initiative to approach Shri. Chandan Singh Barkatia, Managing Director of Malwa Textile Mills and a respected philanthropist, along with Shri. Labhchand Chhajalani, the founder of Nai Dunia Press and a prominent figure in the community. Their support was instrumental in the effort to establish an organization dedicated to the welfare of the blind.

The first meeting for this purpose was convened on May 27, 1959, at the residence of Shri. Chandan Singh Barkatia. During this meeting, it was unanimously decided to form a constitution committee, with me serving as the Convener. I co-opted Advocate Shri. Deshmukh and senior teacher Shri. Jog as members of the committee. For guidance, we referred to the rules and regulations of the Blind Men's Association in Bombay. Using these as a foundation, we drafted the constitution for the "MP Welfare Association for the Blind, Indore."

Under the Chairmanship of Dr. (Mrs.) Bryce, the constitution was formally adopted, and an ad hoc Executive Council was formed in June 1960. Subsequently, the organization was officially registered under the then-existing Firm and Societies Act on December 13, 1960. This marked a significant milestone in establishing the "MP Welfare Association for the Blind."

The association was inaugurated on January 4, 1961, in the Bronzer Hall of Christian College, Indore—a date chosen to honor the birth anniversary of Louis Braille, the inventor of the Braille script. Shri. Youdhister Bhargav, Commissioner of Indore Division, presided over the event, while Dr. R. T. Vyas, the then

Development Officer of NAB India, graced the occasion as the Chief Guest.

At that time, no social organization in Indore was dedicated to the welfare of the blind, making it imperative to raise awareness about this cause. Leveraging Dr. R. T. Vyas's presence, we organized a series of impactful speeches at educational institutions, social organizations, and the Indore Municipal Corporation, successfully spreading awareness and garnering support for the association's objectives.

Initial Days

The inception of the MP Welfare Association for the Blind came as a blessing, not only for me but also for the visually impaired community at the state level. Before the formation of MPWAB, inclusive social development for the visually impaired was nonexistent.

The organization had to undertake a herculean task to open all possible avenues in the shortest time. Parents often ignored the rights of their blind children, educators were hesitant to accept them in regular schools, and there were no special schools to provide education even up to the secondary level. Economic rehabilitation remained nothing more than a distant dream. Ministers would dismissively say that when even able-bodied individuals struggled to find employment, expecting jobs for the visually impaired was unrealistic. The situation turned truly pathetic at times, with educated blind individuals being advised by ministers to sing songs near temples and entertain visitors for a few coins to survive! The fundamental rights of every human being were poorly understood and valued, both by society at large and by politicians and administrators alike.

MP Welfare Association for the Blind came to be seen as an oasis in the desert of the social environment. With the support of a few dedicated and seasoned individuals, we were able to navigate through the harsh sands of neglect and indifference, bringing hope and sustenance to those who needed it most.

Mr. Balkrishna Shah joined me in supporting the organization's effective functioning. A pioneer in social initiatives, he had introduced Rotary Club and Lions Club activities for the first time in Indore. Alongside his involvement in social causes, he was engaged in the business of agricultural equipment, implements, and parts, as well as holding a dealership for Jyoti Pump. His calm demeanor and accommodating nature helped the organization establish firm roots. Before this, he had spent several years working alongside the veteran social worker of Gujarat, popularly known as Thakur Bapa.

Smt. Krishna Agrawal, an eminent social worker in the town, was leading the Bhartiya Grameen Mahila Sangh and was also a member of the MP Social Welfare Board. With her vast experience in working for the downtrodden, she became a valuable asset to the newly formed MPWAB. Her husband, Dr. Ramesh Agrawal, a renowned ophthalmologist, shared her compassion and had a special soft corner for the visually impaired.

Dr. R. P. Dhanda, a distinguished ophthalmologist and Reader at MGM Medical College, Indore, joined the organization with a special focus on eye care. I had the unique advantage of working alongside him at MY Hospital, which allowed for regular communication and easy access to personal discussions whenever needed.

For the first few months, the organization had no dedicated office space. We managed operations from my clinic in the evenings. A part-time typist was hired, and a typewriter was purchased at my expense.

For all these years, I shared the house with my sister-in-law (my brother's wife). My brother mostly stayed in Ujjain at our parental home, visiting us occasionally for a few days.

The Work Begins!

Until 1961, Madhya Pradesh had only two institutions offering primary education for visually challenged children. There were no facilities for secondary education or socio-economic rehabilitation for the visually impaired. Many young individuals faced uncertainty, wandering in search of opportunities for economic rehabilitation without possessing the necessary skills to secure meaningful employment.

To address these challenges, the MP Welfare Association for the Blind (MPWAB) established the Rehabilitation Centre for the Blind in Indore on August 15, 1961.Initially operating from a rented single room, the center focused on providing training in chair caning as a modest income-generating initiative. It began with eight blind youths from the town, who actively participated in the program. Offices brought their chairs to the center for re-caning, creating a small but meaningful source of income.

Shri. Sharad Gandhe, my close friend with low vision, played a pivotal role in managing this activity. After about a year, the center relocated to Pandey Building near Kishanpura Bridge. This new location offered sufficient space for the training unit, as well as lodging and boarding facilities for the trainees.

For a few days, meals were sourced from a local hotel, but eventually, a female cook was hired. The first challenge I faced was, the food from the hotel was discontinued, and the cook failed to show up for nearly a week! I was tasked with providing meals for 7-8 trainees, but with no attendant available, I was helpless! Luckily, my nephew, Mr. Arun Yadvadkar, was with me preparing for his intermediate exams. He rose to the occasion, took over the cooking, and served the trainees for almost a week. His timely help was invaluable and greatly appreciated, as it allowed us to continue running the center. This act of support boosted our morale and enthusiasm significantly.

Over time, the Rehabilitation Centre expanded its services, providing free lodging and boarding to 28 residents. By 1962-63, a Handloom Weaving unit was introduced alongside chair caning as part of vocational training. Recognizing that many residents were unfamiliar with Braille, we also established an Adult Literacy unit. This initiative aimed to teach Braille reading and writing, basic arithmetic, and music as part of skill development.

Shri. Shamsuddin Sheikh, a blind youth, played a significant role in managing this literacy unit. His dedication ensured the effective running of Braille literacy and music classes, contributing immensely to the education and skill enhancement of adult blind individuals at the center.

The MP Welfare Association for the Blind (MPWAB) also initiated a state-level sports meet, which quickly gained popularity and became a regular annual event for several years. This activity not only fostered physical fitness and confidence among visually impaired individuals but also created a platform to showcase their talent and determination.

To raise awareness about our responsibilities towards visually challenged individuals, a state-level workshop was organized in January 1964. Many of the institutions working in this field at the time participated in the event. The workshop was inaugurated by the Governor of Madhya Pradesh, His Excellency Shri. H. V. Pataskar. A souvenir was presented for the first time on this occasion. Despite limited government support and minimal public contributions, the workshop was successfully organized.

Shri. Gaurilal Shukla, the then Director of Social Welfare, attended the inauguration and actively participated in the workshop's discussions. He praised my efforts, though in an ironic tone, calling me "a mad person." Seeing my puzzled expression, he quickly clarified that it was a quote from Shri. Vinobaji: *"A person has to become mad if they want to involve themselves in human services."* This comment was a source of great consolation for me, strengthening my resolve to continue with the mission I held dear.

Awareness about the cause was steadily spreading in society, with individuals of notable standing in the community beginning to contribute actively and offer moral support. In 1962, Dr. R. C. Dhanda, a renowned ophthalmologist, became the president of the organization. Mrs. Krishna Agrawal, a dynamic social worker in the town, joined as vice president, and Shri. Balkrishna Shah, an active Lion, became the treasurer from the organization's inception.

In 1962-63, another energetic social worker, Mrs. Krishna Chawla (wife of the Director of Aakashwani Indore), also joined our efforts. I must also mention Dr. D. L. Golhar, Head of Department of Physiotherapy, who played a key role in the initial years. He graciously extended his services as one of the secretaries of the organization for about a year, providing invaluable support.

Developing a team of dedicated workers has always been a challenging task. Controversies often arise when making mature decisions, especially when financial risks are involved. During such times, one often finds himself in a dilemma and looks for someone to provide guidance.

In those difficult days, Mr. Ganesh Chintaman Tambe, a veteran horticulturist, joined us as a member of the executive council. Shri. Tambe had lost his sight at an advanced age, and this shared experience brought us together for a common cause. His maturity, wealth of experience, and educational background made him not just a colleague, but my friend, philosopher, and guide in navigating various challenges.

The first time I brought up the topic of differing opinions among colleagues, Shri. Tambe calmly assessed the situation and asked, "Do you play chess?" Though I couldn't immediately grasp the relevance of his question, I responded enthusiastically, mentioning that I had played chess with great interest during my childhood.

He then advised me, “In managing the affairs of the organization, you must act like a skilled chess player. You cannot change the behaviour of others, but you can regulate your own actions in response to the situation.” He went on to explain, “Each piece in chess has its fixed movement, and you cannot expect them to move differently. Similarly, people behave in their own ways; you cannot expect them to act exactly as you wish. You must decide when and where to utilize a particular member’s skills and where to keep them in reserve.”

His advice was profound and practical, and I have followed it over the years. It has been a source of comfort and wisdom for me. Shri. Tambe, a classmate of Shri. Vinobaji during their school days in Baroda, offered me invaluable guidance, which I believe holds great relevance in navigating day-to-day interactions and striving toward higher goals in life.

Friendships, for some, endure a lifetime, while for others, they may be shorter-lived—reasons for this variation are countless. Those who remain by our side for the longer stretch are often considered our best friends. Shri. Sharad Gandhe, a visually impaired youth, became one of my closest friends in 1955. We often shared our thoughts and helped each other in decision-making.

Though his eyesight was poor for several years, he was able to navigate independently and occasionally escorted me. I encouraged him to pursue his education and take the matriculation examination. He passed on his first attempt and continued his studies. Apart from being academically inclined, he was also a talented violinist and served at the government music college in Indore.

Sharad was a dedicated member of our organization, serving as an executive member and later as Hon. Secretary for two consecutive terms of three years each. His loyalty, commitment, and friendship have been invaluable over the years.

Massive Upgradation of Rehabilitation Training Center!

Since the inception of the M.P. Welfare Association for the Blind (MPWAB), we were determined to develop comprehensive, "need-based-training" for the visually impaired. The increasing scope of our activities made it clear that we could no longer operate from a rented building. Therefore, in 1968, we acquired a piece of land in Laxmibai Nagar Industrial Estate. While securing the land, we worked tirelessly to raise funds and secure a grant-in-aid from the Government of India. Shri. Balkrishna Shah, the then treasurer of our organization, played a key role in persuading the Lions Club of Indore to contribute funds for the construction of a sheltered workshop. The Lions Club generously donated Rs. 25,000. With this initial contribution, we were able to approach the Government of India, who subsequently provided Rs. 1,50,000. By the end of December 1970, the workshop building was completed.

I was particularly eager to have the Vice President of India inaugurate the workshop. To our delight, Shri. Gopal Swaroop Pathak, the then Vice President of India, graciously accepted our invitation and inaugurated the workshop on 1st February 1971. This marked a significant milestone in our mission to improve the lives of the visually impaired.

After the inauguration, the Light Engineering Unit was established within the workshop-cum-rehabilitation center. We equipped the unit with all the necessary industrial training machines, providing the visually impaired with essential skills to enter the workforce.

In order to expand the placement opportunities for deserving blind youths, a dedicated officer was appointed at MPWAB, marking the first such initiative in Madhya Pradesh. This step was highly appreciated by the community and government officials alike. Shri. B. K. Sokal and Shri. Ramesh Bakare, the Placement Officers at MPWAB, worked tirelessly and wholeheartedly to facilitate placements for blind youths. Additionally, Shri. Arun Modi, a young Placement Officer from the National Association for the Blind, M.P. State Branch, played a significant role in securing placements for blind youths in reputed corporate establishments. This effort greatly enhanced the visibility and employment prospects of visually impaired individuals in various professional sectors.

The Rehabilitation Centre developed rapidly as it became the only one of its kind in northern India, providing training and preparing visually impaired individuals for appropriate and gainful employment. Candidates from various states, including Rajasthan, Gujarat, Uttar Pradesh, Bihar, Orissa, and Maharashtra, also enrolled at the Centre to benefit from its light engineering training. It opened doors to job opportunities in large-scale industries and public sector undertakings, including BHEL, Government Paper Security Mills, and the Ordinance Factory, among others.

BHEL Bhopal absorbed more than 10 visually impaired youths into their large establishment. One of these employees later received the prestigious SHRAM SHREE AWARD from the Government of India for his exceptional productivity. This remarkable achievement not only highlighted the capabilities of visually impaired individuals but also encouraged other industries to hire trained blind youths, expanding employment opportunities for them.

During those years, a significant number of visually impaired youths were employed in various textile mills in Mumbai. Inspired by this success, I decided to approach local textile mills to create similar opportunities for blind individuals in our region. I visited several industries in Mumbai and sought support from Shri. Vijay Merchant to pursue local textile authorities in this direction. After persistent efforts, Malwa Mill authorities agreed to hire two blind workers at a monthly salary of Rs.50 each, while the normal workers were earning Rs.150-250 per month.

I advised these two blind youths not to quit their jobs under any circumstances, as their employment would pave the way for more blind individuals to secure jobs in other textile mills. Over time, our efforts bore fruit. More local textile mills in Indore and Heera Mills in Ujjain followed suit, employing 10 blind individuals, expanding employment opportunities in the region.

It is also noteworthy that some of the trained blind youths ventured into self-employment as exceptional means of livelihood. One such individual, Mr. Laxman Chouhan, established his own small-scale plastic industry, eventually employing normal workers in his business. Others engaged in self-employment as hawkers, managing sales in railway compartments, going door-to-door, or selling goods in busy marketplaces.

Thus, MPWAB played a leading and pioneering role in securing job opportunities for the visually impaired in Madhya Pradesh. Over time, government establishments, banks, and corporate sectors developed greater awareness about the economic rehabilitation of the blind and grew confident in their skills.

This shift marked a significant transformation in societal attitudes. The perception of the blind began to change at an appreciable level, as society no longer viewed them as beggars but as dignified individuals capable of contributing meaningfully. The efforts of MPWAB helped foster this cultural shift and promoted the social and economic rehabilitation of the blind, bringing them into the mainstream workforce with respect and recognition.

***

Chapter 8

Personal Challenges

"Go within every day and find the inner strength so that the world will not blow your candle out."

-Katherine Dunham.

They say calamities never come alone, often arriving in relentless succession. Before one can recover from one blow, another strikes. My life, too, seemed overshadowed by such a series of misfortunes. The loss of sight in childhood, compounded by the deprivation of parental love and affection, loomed large over my formative years. There were moments when events and circumstances turned so harsh that I questioned the purpose of life itself. At that tender age, it felt as if every door to progress and development had been shut firmly against me.

Elder Brother's Schizophrenia

While I was beginning to find some solace in building my career, life once again presented me with profound challenges. My elder brother Dattatraya began to exhibit symptoms of schizophrenia—a condition that would profoundly affect not just him, but our entire family.

He was undergoing training as a professional wireless operator at Koni, Bilaspur, when he began to first exhibit its symptoms. The first alarming sign was a letter from him stating that someone had set fire to our house in Ujjain and that tenants were destroying it—claims that had absolutely no basis in reality. His reactions and responses to imaginary scenarios deeply worried me.

Recognizing the gravity of the situation, I urged him to come to Bombay without delay. During his brief visit to Bombay, I observed his erratic behavior, which confirmed my fears about his mental health. He spoke of being hypnotized, convinced that he had lost control over his thoughts and actions. In an attempt to understand his condition, he delved into books on hypnotism, but instead of providing clarity, it only worsened his state.

He sought psychiatric treatment in Indore and Gwalior, which brought some temporary relief. In the meantime, he secured a position in the anti-locus unit of the Postal Department in Jodhpur and got married in 1955. Both he and his wife relocated to Jodhpur, while I was establishing my physiotherapy practice in Indore.

Despite initial stability, his condition began to deteriorate again. He consulted a local psychiatrist in Jodhpur and started medication, but the improvement was short-lived. A tragic incident soon followed. I received a telegram from his house owner, urgently calling me to Jodhpur. Upon my arrival, I learned that my brother had suffered a severe psychotic episode, assaulting his wife throughout the night. The situation escalated to the point where the police had to intervene and break open the door.

Under the circumstances, the police admitted him to a mental hospital. His wife, left distraught and alone, awaited my arrival. With no other option, we packed their belongings and brought her back to Indore, where she could find support and care. This series of events left a profound impact on all of us, underscoring the devastating effects of untreated mental illness on individuals and families alike.

After a few weeks of his release from the mental hospital, my brother came to Indore. We attempted to keep him and his wife with us, hoping that family support might help stabilize his condition. However, his episodes of fury became unpredictable and dangerous—he would lash out and assault any of us without provocation.

In our relentless efforts to help him, we sought further treatment at Gwalior Mental Hospital. He was diagnosed to have disorganized schizophrenia, previously known as hebephrenic schizophrenia. His symptoms were:

(a) Delusions, where he held unshakable but false beliefs.

(b) Somatic hallucinations, where he experienced false perceptions related to his body.

(c) Hallucinations, including vivid sensory experiences that had no basis in reality.

(d) Hearing voices, often commenting on or criticizing his actions.

(e) Thought insertion or withdrawal, where he believed external forces were controlling his thoughts.

Tragically, he escaped from the hospital and returned to his violent ways. Managing his condition became increasingly challenging. Ultimately, we decided to send him to Ujjain, where he stayed with our brother-in-law and cousin sister.

At Ujjain, his condition continued to worsen. He withdrew completely, isolating himself in a room where he spent most of his time sleeping. This grim existence persisted until October 1964, when he passed away.

To witness Dattatreya's eleven-year battle with schizophrenia was one of the most harrowing chapters of my life. His suffering was heartbreaking to witness. The constant fear, helplessness, and exhaustion were indescribable. It left him socially withdrawn and vulnerable.

We tried our best to take care of him, but in the end, it was as if nature, in its own painful way, intervened to bring this tragic episode to full stop.

Lung Infection

Around 1964-65, I also contracted a lung infection and had to undergo prolonged treatment for more than six months. Dr. KantilalHawaldar, provided immense support during my treatment. I knew Dr. Kantilal personally and also his father earlier. During this difficult time, I was blessed with the dedicated service of Shri. Ram Joshi, a teenager who served me with complete dedication. The tender care I received from Mrs. Leela Taai Narolikar and Ram Joshi helped me recover from the deadly lung infection.

At times, I reflect on how people with absolutely no blood relation can extend support without any expectations, compared to close blood, who don't even care! It makes me believe that this is what we call the karma of a previous birth. I am deeply grateful to Almighty God for sending such wonderful helpful people into my life—people who understood me, loved me, supported me, encouraged me, and helped lead me toward my goal.

Outside Food

Later, my sister-in-law, who was also residing within the premises of our organization due to the health condition of my brother Dattatreya, left the organization. Being alone without active company took a toll on my mental well-being, especially because I had to rely on meals from outside. The food from various restaurants did not suit my body and led to colitis and other abdominal issues. From 1962 to 1967, I was at the mercy of outside food.

Then Smt. Leela Narolikar who had a sisterly bond with me, came to my rescue and offered me home-cooked meals every day, personally delivering them through one of her sons. Her kindness and care provided me with much-needed comfort during a time of hardship.

From January 1968 until my marriage in June 1968, I arranged for a female cook to prepare meals for me at my residence, which provided some relief to both my taste and my health. Despite these challenging and stressful times, I remained committed to my duties at the hospital and the MP Welfare Association for the Blind, ensuring that my responsibilities were always attended to with sincerity.

Younger Brother's Schizophrenia

My younger brother Chandrakant had been building a promising career as a Sales Representative for Siemens India, specializing in medical electronic equipment. He was not only successful in his professional life but also seemed content in his personal life, living happily with his wife and two children. But then, his life took a sudden and unfortunate turn.

Workplace disagreements with his seniors escalated into a full-blown controversy, ultimately leading to the loss of his job. The shock of this event was devastating for him, and it triggered the onset of schizophrenia. Over time, his condition worsened, with delusions taking over his thoughts and behavior. These delusions distanced him from friends, family, and society.

As a professional counselor, I tried everything I could to help him. I spent months counseling him, attempting to guide him out of the fantasies that had overtaken his mind. Despite my efforts, his condition showed no improvement. Tragically, our relationship deteriorated to the point where he began avoiding me entirely.

Chandrakant's illness caused a complete rupture in his personal life as well. He divorced his first wife and now lives with his second wife in near-total isolation. Though he remains distant,

I often think about him, hoping for some semblance of peace in his life despite the formidable challenges he continues to face.

In moments of reflection, I often ponder the unpredictable nature of life. It feels like an unending chain of struggles, each link forged in hardship and uncertainty. Yet, amidst this storm, I find solace in the belief that those who endure such challenges are also granted strength and patience by the Almighty. This divine support, I believe, enables us to persevere and rise above adversity, though only when nature deems the time right.

***

Chapter 9

Marriage

"Marriage is a narrative of God taking two people on an adventure through a life that ultimately leads to eternity."

-Anonymous

In the primitive age, there were neither families nor a marriage system. Nomadic men and women moved from place to place in search of food, fulfilling biological needs through short-term mutual understandings. Conflicts often arose over life partners.

Over time, as people settled along riverbanks and engaged in agriculture, they began to recognize the importance of family. This realization led to stable lives and marked the transformation of humans into social animals.

While accepting this concept, society has given little thought to those who remain unmarried throughout their lives, whether due to circumstances forced upon them by physical, mental, or other conditions, or by their voluntary decision to live alone. Many choose not to marry simply because they prefer to avoid the responsibilities of family life.

Family, as we understand it, involves living happily together, sharing responsibilities, and enjoying mutual rights for the well-being of each member. However, many *sadhus* live solitary lives within groups, relying on the mercy *gurus*. Physical and mental disabilities, chronic illnesses, extreme poverty, and similar factors can also compel people to remain alone throughout their lives.

You might wonder how a visually impaired, completely blind person could marry and take on the responsibilities of a family, or how they could raise children. I, too, was quite apprehensive about it. The attitude of society was far from supportive or sensitive to the needs of the visually impaired in this regard.

During my schooling years from 1949 to 1955, I observed the lives of several blind individuals deprived of married life. Two of our blind teachers, proficient in their respective subjects and economically self-sufficient, remained bachelors throughout their lives as parents were unwilling to accept them as suitable bridegrooms. However, they managed to stay unmarried as they lived in joint families. Similarly, some blind teachers from the Happy Home School for the Blind were provided accommodation within the institution itself, leading them to live solitary lives in the organization's hostel.

Mr. Baburao Kadam, a blind teacher previously introduced in this book as a palmist, had numerous male and female clients seeking insights into their future and solutions to their problems. Some girls even approached him to inquire about the likelihood of a successful marriage. However, none of these girls ever considered marrying this financially independent blind man.

Similarly, another teacher, Mr. Gokul Das Joshi, an exceptional musician highly admired by music enthusiasts in the community, faced a similar predicament. Even girls with a passion for music never considered choosing the talented blind musician as their life partner.

Mr. and Mrs. Alpaiwala were the first couple I came across where Mr. Alpaiwala was blind, and his wife was a sighted woman. Barrister R. M. Alpaiwala, who suffered from retinitis pigmentosa, likely lost his vision later in life after living a family life for many years.

Another inspiring example is Ms. Suvarna, a highly educated sighted woman, who married Mr. Suresh Ahuja, an equally well-educated blind man. Their marriage, built on mutual understanding, allowed them to lead a fulfilling family life until Mr. Ahuja's passing. Together, they served the visually impaired community professionally for over 30 years, earning national respect and recognition.

Similarly, Dr. R. T. Vyas, a completely blind man with a dynamic personality, married Madhuri, the daughter of film director Mr. Ramchandra Thakur, in 1959. This union was highly admired in Mumbai at the time. Madhuri's sacrifices earned her a unique status and deep respect within society, particularly among the blind community. During those days, blindness was considered a social stigma, posing a significant barrier to marriage for many visually impaired individuals.

I was not an exception to this social stigma. One common reality in most cases is that the family members of blind individuals often show little interest in pursuing their marriage. Instead, their primary focus tends to be on the blind person's earnings, which become a significant source for the family's financial upkeep. I experienced this attitude from my own family throughout those years.

By 1964, I had completed 32 years of my life without finding a solution to having a life partner to marry. Alongside my job and my voluntary services as Honorary Secretary of MPWAB for the visually impaired, I was also dedicated to my private physiotherapy practice. At the same time, I was pursuing my graduation. My readers would read textbooks to me, and I would take a few notes in Braille.

Neelam

One day, a young girl Neelam agreed to work as my reader for about a year. She would read for me for two hours a day with complete dedication. Over time, she seemed to develop a certain fascination for me, and I responded to it. One day, while reading my textbooks, she abruptly stopped and fell silent. Despite my repeated questions about what had happened, she didn't respond immediately, remaining quiet for several moments.

I couldn't understand what was wrong and felt a bit perturbed. Concerned, I moved closer, patted her on the shoulder, and gently asked her the reason for her silence. She was trembling, and I too became emotionally disturbed. It was the first experience of its kind for me. After a minute or two, she cleared her throat and, with a choked voice, spoke, "I was thinking about you—the way you work so hard despite your blindness, your zeal and motivation to complete your graduation, your profession, and your voluntary services for the blind. It moved me deeply."

"So what?" I asked her.

She hesitated for a moment before replying, "If you had been a sighted person, you would have achieved so much more and reached an even higher position in society."

Without much thought, I responded, "Can you share your eyes and mental support to help me achieve my goals?"

"I will do my best," she said.

Reading sessions continued as usual. About a week later, during one of our daily textbook sessions, I offered her an orange and suggested taking a short break. She was seated on her chair, and I was on my cot. Once again, she became silent. I tried to persuade her to accept the orange, but her response was subdued.

I stood up, walked over to her chair, and handed her the orange. At that moment, I realized I needed to muster some boldness. Summoning all my courage, I asked her, "If you feel such affinity for me, would you like to marry me?"

She remained silent, tears welling up in her eyes. The question moved her deeply, and it seemed to strengthen the bond we had begun to share!

A couple of days later, she finally accepted. "I have decided to marry you," she said. However, she added, after some days, "I will need to seek the consent of my parents and brothers."

After that incident, she began dedicating more time to reading the study material for me. Her fascination and affection towards me seemed to grow stronger with each passing day. This was during 1963-64, and with her unwavering support, I continued my studies and successfully cleared my examination!

After my examination, Neelam and I began making efforts to finalize the date for our marriage, and she worked diligently to gain her family's consent. While her parents agreed, her brothers became resistant and even violent. They sent her to Gwalior to stay with their elder sister. It was a distressing time for me, and in my desperation to understand the situation, I followed her to Gwalior with a few close well-wishers. At my request, she came to the hotel where I was staying, and we had lunch together. Once again, she reassured me that her decision to marry me was unwavering.

A few days after her return to Indore, she visited me unexpectedly. After a moment of silence, she shared that her elder brother remained adamantly opposed to our union and had even instructed their parents not to let her leave the house. This revelation was a devastating blow for me. The situation was unbearable, leaving me with no option but to confront a deadlock.

In light of these recent developments, I moved to a rented flat, leaving behind the hostel and institution. Many nights were spent sleepless on the terrace of that flat, enduring a unique and sorrowful phase of my life. I cannot clearly recall how I eventually regained the mental strength to return to my daily activities as before.

One evening in December 1966, to my surprise, Neelam came to my clinic and informed me that she was going to marry someone else in two days. I congratulated her and wished her a happy married life. She went on to say that her best wishes would always be with me and that, emotionally, she would remain connected to me. She added, "Neither will I die, nor will I allow you to die."

With those words, Neelam left—and left me forever.

Meena

Mrs. Krishna Agrawal, an eminent social worker and Vice-President of our organization, learned about the distressing episode I had gone through. Determined to help, she began looking for a suitable match for me. In 1967, she called me to her residence, where a girl from Jabalpur was present. Mrs. Agrawal introduced her, saying, "She is Meena, she has completed her matriculation and is currently studying nursing in Ujjain. She lost her parents in the violent riots last year and is now under my care. If you both mutually consent, you may consider this match. Take her to your home, discuss openly, and let her decide."

We went to my home and had an earnest conversation about the possibility of marriage. Meena agreed but expressed her desire to complete her nursing training first, which would take about a year and a half. She asked me to wait until then. Over the following months, we met briefly two or three times, keeping our promise alive.

Shobha

While waiting for Meena to complete her nursing, an interesting proposal came my way. One of my friends, Shri. Vamanrao Pathak, a blind-trained teacher from Nagpur, approached me one day. He mentioned that he had a niece and, if I was open to it, he could discuss the possibility of marriage with her parents. He did, however, point out that his niece wasn't highly educated. He strongly urged me to visit Nagpur to meet her in person. Since I had known him for some time, I decided to consider the offer.

In May 1968, I had to attend a conference in Calcutta, which required a long journey from Mumbai. Coincidentally, Mr. Pathak and his wife were also attending the same conference. They suggested that I make a stop at Nagpur for 10–12 hours before continuing onward to Calcutta.

I started the journey accompanied by Shri. Dwarka Prasad, who was serving as Superintendent in the organization.

As suggested, we took a stop at Nagpur to meet the girl and her family. At 20 years of age, Ms. Shobha was the second child of her parents. Due to financial constraints, her father, who worked in the railway mail service on a modest salary, could barely afford to provide his children with a primary education. After having lunch with them, we resumed our journey to Calcutta. During the journey, Shri. Pathak and his wife persistently encouraged me to marry their niece.

The conference we attended was the second gathering of the National Association for the Instructors for the Blind, held at Narendrapur, where the Blind Boys' Academy was situated. The academy, run by the Ramakrishna Mission, was an impressive institution with a beautifully maintained garden, a well-equipped auditorium, a light engineering unit, and a school for the blind. Our three-day stay was both enriching and inspiring. We returned with new knowledge and a renewed sense of purpose and energy.

In the third week of June 1968, without prior notice, Mr. and Mrs. Pathak arrived in Indore with their niece Shobha for final discussions with my uncle and other family members. Despite the short notice, arrangements were made, and we got married in a simple ceremony on June 23, 1968.

For me, it was a crucial and difficult decision. Shobha's educational background had not met my expectations, but I had accepted the proposal with mixed emotions, deeply empathizing with her dire circumstances which had prevailed on her side.

As I stood at this turning point, a quotation lingered in my mind: "Love is the dawn of marriage, and marriage is the sunset of life." I also reflected on Bernard Shaw's words: "Those who marry, they repent, and those who do not marry, they also repent." Until the age of 36, I had lived the first part of this sentiment as a chronic bachelor, enduring the frustration and social stigma of delayed marriage. Now, I was stepping into the second part, facing the reality of a marriage fraught with initial maladjustment.

After our marriage, we took steps to bridge the gaps between us. Shobha was enrolled in adult literacy classes at Shramik Vidyapeeth for several months. We also arranged private tutoring for her for over a year to enhance her reading and writing skills. Gradually, over the years, we embarked on a long and arduous journey of mutual adjustment.

Birth of our Daughter

August 1970 marked a profoundly auspicious milestone in our lives with the birth of our daughter Jyotsna. Her arrival felt like a divine blessing, ushering in prosperity and joy in the years that followed. In her, I saw the image of my mother, a comforting presence that strengthened me in countless ways. Jyotsna has been a pillar of support, her unwavering love and care becoming a source of endless strength and solace in my journey.

As I pen this part of my autobiography, I can look back and say that we have reached a place of reasonable harmony and deep understanding. Today, I am convinced of the age-old belief: "Marriage, birth, and death are decided in heaven!"

Furthermore, I have come to realize that marriage is a romance where the hero dies in the first chapter. It is equally true that it is a battlefield, not a bed of roses. During my sociology studies, my professor Dr. Abraham often quoted, "For a successful married life, the husband should be partially deaf and the wife partially blind." In our case, everything seemed reversed—I live my life without sight, while in the early years, my partner was inattentive, as if she were partially deaf!

A happy marriage is truly the union of two good forgivers. Today, I no longer face these challenges, as she has become vigilant in both mind and sight, guiding us through our daily lives. It is a beautiful thing to see a husband and wife grow together, rediscovering love along the way.

That is what marriage truly means—helping one another reach the fullest potential as responsible, autonomous individuals who don't run away from life. Matrimony is like a vast ocean for which no compass has yet been invented. Therefore, it is the mind, not the body, that sustains a lasting marriage.

***

Chapter 10

My Family – A Social Help desk

"Never stop doing little things for others. Sometimes those little things occupy the biggest part of their hearts and shower on us as blessings of God."

-Anonymous

I refer to my family as a "Social Help desk" in its broader sense. My family has equally played an active role in helping friends and others find life partners. I'll share two unique and interesting examples to illustrate this.

One such case was that of Shri. Sharad Gandhe, a close friend of mine who, being visually impaired, faced difficulties in settling down with a life partner. He had four brothers who were well settled, but none of them took the initiative to find a suitable match for him. At the time, we had a South Indian tenant, Ms. Laxmi Aiyangar, a Tamil girl, who often visited us. She had developed a friendly relationship with my family. The Aiyangar family had three brothers and two sisters; the eldest brother chose to live a bachelor life, and the elder sister was suffering from a chronic illness. As a result, the family was in disarray, and no one cared for Ms. Laxmi's marriage prospects.

Ms. Laxmi eventually confided in my wife, expressing her frustration about her situation. My wife, moved by her story, offered to help her settle her matrimony. We suggested that Ms. Laxmi consider Shri. Sharad Gandhe as a potential match, even though he was blind. After a week or two of thoughtful consideration, she accepted the proposal. We then convinced Shri. Sharad Gandhe to consider Ms. Laxmi as his life partner, and with time, even his father agreed.

Their marriage was settled through our timely initiative and persistence. Today, they are happily married with a daughter who has grown up, completed her MBA, and is happily married herself. She is now working in a well-reputed company in Jaipur.

Shri. Munnalal Sharma, a blind music instructor who worked with us, was also seeking a suitable match for himself. After some time, we came across a Punjabi girl from a distressed family. She was skilled in multiple crafts and also had special catering skills. We brought them together and arranged their marriage in a warm and cordial atmosphere. Today, they are happily married, living in harmony, and enjoying a life of mutual respect and care for each other.

Apart from supporting education, livelihood, and matrimonial issues, my family and I were always there for those in need of hospitalization due to long illnesses. It was unusual in the sense that there were closer relatives, yet they couldn't manage to provide the proper personal care for their loved ones. As a social laboratory, my family and I took great pleasure in making others happy by fulfilling their needs. I can confidently say that I have earned nothing but the blessings of those who were in need, stressed, and struggling to find their way. I simply offered them my hand, strengthened them, and tried to give back to society what I had always strived for.

***

Chapter 11

MPWAB Completes a Decade of Service!

"A river cuts through rock, not because of its power, but because of its persistence."

-Jim Watkins

As our organization, M.P.W.A.B., celebrated a decade of service to the cause of the visually impaired, we worked on planning the decennial celebrations in 1971. One of the most exciting and groundbreaking activities for this occasion was the first-ever Chess and Swimming tournaments for the blind, held at a national level.

This was a pioneering venture, as no other organization had undertaken such an initiative at the national level before. While blind individuals had been playing chess for years in India, and many were skilled swimmers, their abilities often went unrecognized by the wider society. Our goal was to bring these talents to the forefront, showcasing the capabilities of visually impaired people in these areas, and to inspire the community to see them beyond their limitations.

In January 1971, we decided to move forward with organizing the unique national Chess and Swimming tournaments for the blind. Despite the significant shortage of manpower and funding, which were major concerns, my drive for innovation and addressing the specific needs of the visually impaired pushed me to take the lead and make this venture a reality.

I was fortunate to have the support of two dedicated volunteers: Shri. Laxman Bhawar, my classmate from post-graduate studies, and my cousin Shri. Vishwanath Shirdhonkar. Their encouragement was invaluable in helping me implement the idea. With their help, we managed to secure entries for the competitions—45 participants for swimming and 24 for the chess event. Although the resources were limited, the passion and commitment of those involved made this national meet a significant milestone in our efforts to showcase the capabilities of the blind community.

Organizing the Swimming Tournament at "Taran Pushkar" presented a significant challenge for us. The Indore Municipal Corporation authorities were initially reluctant to allow such an event, citing concerns about potential life hazards. To overcome this obstacle, we sought the support of Shri. Laxmansingh Chouhan, who was then the Chairman of the Swimmers Association. Shri. Chouhan took a bold stand, assuring the corporation authorities that he would take full responsibility for the event. His efforts were instrumental in gaining approval.

The cooperation from the swimming instructors at Taran Pushkar was invaluable. Not only did they agree to oversee the competition, but they also dedicated time to helping local blind swimmers practice in various events. Their commitment to ensuring the swimmers were well-prepared for the competition added tremendous value to the event. With this collective support, we were able to move forward with the swimming tournament, marking an important milestone in our mission to highlight and showcase the remarkable talents of the visually impaired.

The next challenge was to find an experienced coach and mentor who could help organize this tournament specifically for the blind. Additionally, local blind youths required some short-term training to familiarize themselves with the rules and regulations of chess competitions. Our search led us to Shri. Vitthal Palsikar, a veteran chess player known for his expertise and involvement in managing chess tournaments in Indore. While he had no prior experience working with blind chess players, he took a great interest in our unique competition. Shri. Palsikar committed to training the local blind chess players for 10 days, helping them prepare for the event.

Now, we had to arrange lodging and boarding facilities for the participants and members, close to the venue of the swimming pool. The Principal of Vaishnav Polytechnic College was generous enough to offer the institution's hostel for accommodation. People in the town took a great interest in this tournament, and widespread publicity was given to these unique competitions. The events gained attention at the national level as well, highlighting the significance of the initiative and the talents of visually impaired individuals in both swimming and chess.

The event was a tremendous success, receiving an overwhelming response and appreciation at both the state and national levels. It not only raised awareness about the potential of visually impaired individuals but also encouraged people to offer them equal opportunities. As a result of this tournament, other organizations began to replicate and organize similar events, particularly chess tournaments. However, swimming competitions have yet to become a regular annual activity at the national level. It remains a field that needs more initiative from the organizers of agencies for the blind. On a positive note, the Blind

Relief Association in New Delhi has formed the National Sports Association for the Blind, which has been conducting annual sports meets for the past few years, ensuring continued engagement for visually impaired athletes.

***

Chapter 12

My 1st Foreign Trip!

"Everything you've ever wanted is on the other side of fear."

- George Addair

In May 1972, the World Council for the Blind organized an international conference on the placement of visually impaired individuals in East Berlin. To my astonishment and delight, I received a letter from the National Association for the Blind (India) informing me that my name had been proposed as part of the Indian delegation for this prestigious event. This recognition filled me with immense joy and served as a profound source of inspiration, reaffirming my dedication to a cause I had passionately pursued for over a decade.

The Indian delegation comprised notable individuals including Capt. H. M. Desai, the General Secretary, Mr. R. T. Vyas, then Development Officer, Mr. Piloo Khambata, Chairman of the Placement Committee, Mrs. Remut Pajalbhoy, and Brigadier Brijesh. Together, we represented India at this international forum. The German organization for the blind generously sponsored our air tickets and other expenses, making the journey even more memorable and impactful.

Being my first visit to the Western world, I was eager to explore and learn from some of the leading institutions in West Germany and the UK. Before departing India, I reached out to the British Council with a request to facilitate a ten-day visit to the UK. To my delight, they graciously accepted, arranging for me to visit major organizations working in the field and managing my stay in London.

Additionally, Dr. Sontag, the Chairman of the War Blind Association of West Germany, extended his support by organizing a one-week visit to West Germany.

There was no direct flight from Mumbai to East Berlin, so we had a layover in Cairo for a few hours before boarding our next flight. With ample time at hand, we seized the opportunity to visit the Pyramids, explore Cairo Tower, and admire the Nile River!

London

After attending the conference in Berlin, I flew to London. The British Council arranged for a tour guide who guided me to the Indian YMCA on Ridge Street, where I stayed for ten days. Each day was packed with visits to various institutions, as meticulously planned by the British Council. Bhau Saheb Kibe of Indore had provided me with a letter of introduction to Shri. Appapant, the Indian Ambassador to the UK. During my visit, I conveyed Bhau Saheb's regards and shared details of my mission.

While in London, I visited the Royal National Institute for the Blind, located near the Indian YMCA. My focus was on their school for partially sighted children and the industrial workshop. Additionally, I toured Blenheim, the birthplace of Mr. Churchill, and visited Oxford University along with other historic landmarks on the return journey to London.

I spent a day with Shri. Madan Lal Khandelwal, a veteran social worker from India who had settled in the UK and was engaged in the tourism business. We spent several hours together, during which I also met some other Indian friends. Shri. Vasavada, who had been associated with us as the Joint Secretary of the organization, provided me with a letter of introduction to his Gujarati friend, who kindly visited me at the Indian YMCA.

Meeting Neelam, Again!

During our brief interaction, I discovered that the person who met me was working in the same electronic industry as Neelam – the same Neelam with whom I had planned to marry but had met with great opposition from her adamant brother! I requested him to convey my message, asking her to contact me if possible. To my delight, on the third morning, I received her call. Overwhelmed with emotion, we exchanged heartfelt updates about our lives. She shared that she was now a mother to a young girl. I invited her to visit me at the Indian YMCA, but she explained that the distance from her residence made it difficult to accept my request. We exchanged warm wishes and concluded our conversation. It was an extraordinary moment—one I never imagined would occur, especially in a foreign land. Life has a way of offering unexpected, unforgettable surprises!

Dr. Munjal

While I was at the breakfast table one morning, a woman approached me with a cheerful greeting and asked, "Do you know me?" It was a moment that tested my memory and presence of mind. Without hesitation, I responded, "Yes, you are Dr. Munjal." She was delighted by my reply. Dr. Munjal had worked for a few years at MY Hospital during her post-graduation in Pediatrics. After marrying, she had left Indore for Jaipur, where she joined the Medical College and eventually became a professor in the Pediatrics department. She mentioned that she was currently on an educational tour under the World Health Organization's program. It had been nearly eight years since she left Indore, and it might have been challenging for most blind to recognize someone after such a long time—but perhaps I had a knack for such things!

Germany

After spending ten days in London, I departed for Cologne, West Germany. My visit was arranged to include several agencies for the blind, thanks to the efforts of Dr. Sontag, President of the War Blind Association of West Germany. Upon arrival at the airport, I was warmly received by two female social workers who escorted me to the hotel. It was evening when I reached, so I settled in to spend the night there before beginning the planned visits the following day.

The next morning, I was informed that I needed to travel to Belborough. A guide escorted me to the railway station and helped me board the train heading there. Unlike the crowded trains in India, this one was relatively empty, with only a few students in my coach. At each station, just one or two passengers would board or disembark.

I faced a challenge communicating with the passengers about whether the train had reached my destination, as the language barrier with Dutch speakers led to cold responses. However, a young man who spoke English reassured me. He explained that the train's last stop was my destination and that someone would meet me there.

When I alighted at the final station, a man approached and introduced himself. He then escorted me to the Rehabilitation Centre for the Blind. This facility, originally established for those who had lost their eyesight during the World War II, had later opened its doors to civilians.

The visit was an eye-opening experience. Among the individuals I encountered was a young man who had lost his forearms. Through skilled corrective surgery, he had been trained to use the ends of his forearms to learn Braille stenography, exemplifying the remarkable potential of human adaptability and determination.

My Experience with "Turkey"

When we arrived at the Rehabilitation Centre around 1 p.m., a few senior staff members greeted me warmly and showed me to my room. They quickly led me to the dining area, and I informed them that I was a strict vegetarian, requesting that only vegetarian food be served. They brought me rice with fruit salad and other accompaniments.

Before taking a bite, I double-checked to confirm the food was purely vegetarian! As I attempted to eat a morsel of rice, I found it impossible to swallow and rushed to the washbasin to spit it out. This moment was both surprising for me and for the serving staff. I returned to the table and asked them to clarify what had been served. They informed me that the rice contained Turkey.

Turkey? Wasn't it supposed to be a country? Confused, I asked them to explain what "Turkey" was. They told me it was a bird, similar to a hen, and commonly consumed in their country. I was taken aback and asked, "How can this be considered vegetarian food?!" They responded, "We consider Turkey a vegetarian food."

Shocked, I kindly requested that they refrain from serving me such "vegetarian" food, as it was clearly not suitable for my dietary needs. For the next two days, the staff took extra care to ensure my meals were properly prepared.

Hosted by a German Family

Since I couldn't speak Dutch, communication often became challenging for those interacting with me. The following day, I was introduced to a German family, and to my relief, they were English-speaking. This connection brought me both comfort and good company.

The family consisted of a husband and wife, forming a close-knit household. I couldn't determine whether they had children or not. The wife was a homemaker, while the husband worked as a physician, typically on duty until the evening.

Joining them was Ms. Inga, a young woman who seemed to be a close friend of the family.

It was lunchtime, so we shared a meal together, which, thankfully, was purely vegetarian. The couple expressed keen interest in learning about Indian culture, the political landscape, Mahatma Gandhi, Smt. Indira Gandhi, the newly-formed Bangladesh and various other aspects of India.

Later in the evening, the lady of the house suggested that I explore the city with her friend, Ms. Inga, for a few hours and return by 8 p.m. Ms. Inga took me out in her car, and we visited a restaurant. After spending about an hour and a half enjoying snacks and conversation, we returned. That night, the physician, who had come back from work, kindly dropped me off at my hotel.

The Rehabilitation Centre, where I stayed for two days, was well-equipped with extensive facilities for skill development and recreation. It boasted amenities like a large swimming pool and a fully functional gymnasium for the beneficiaries. Known as SPA, the center was widely recognized in Germany for its state-of-the-art therapeutic equipment. These resources were designed to help users rejuvenate their physical and mental energy, enabling them to return to their jobs with renewed vigor and vitality.

That evening, around 8:30 p.m., dinner was served, and I joined others at the dining table. Ms. Inga was present too as she had relatives in Marlborough. She had planned to join them for dinner and stay for the night at their house, hence she couldn't join me at my table. However, after I finished, she kindly escorted me to my room, ensured I was comfortable, and then departed for her relatives' place.

The next morning, during breakfast, I was pleasantly surprised to see Ms. Inga arrive at the Centre to meet me. Though we offered her breakfast, she politely declined and only had a cup of coffee while sitting with me at the dining table. Before leaving, she handed me a thoughtful gift—a coffee pot—which I gratefully accepted, expressing my heartfelt thanks for her kind gesture. She then accompanied me to my room, before departing. Later in the evening, I traveled to Marlborough, preparing for my visit to the renowned Marlborough School for the Blind scheduled for the following day.

Marlborough School for the Blind

Marlborough School for the Blind was not an academic institution but a manufacturing hub for a wide range of Braille equipment, including the renowned Marlborough Brailler. I spent several hours there, closely observing their activities, which were impressively focused on addressing the educational needs of blind children and youth. Their efforts left a lasting impression on me. Later in the evening, I returned to my room, reflecting on the impactful work being carried out at that organisation.

After about an hour, I heard a knock at my door. It was a blind youth from Iran who had come to Germany to complete his graduation, drawn by the superior educational opportunities available there. We engaged in a casual conversation, discussing various social and political issues concerning our respective countries. His perspectives were intriguing, and the exchange was both enlightening and thought-provoking. After some time, he bid me goodbye and left the room.

Mines City

By evening, I reached Mines City and checked into a hotel for the night. Over the past two days, I hadn't been able to take a bath as there were no attached bathrooms at the accommodations I stayed in, including the Belzberg Rehabilitation Centre. At the hotel in Mines City, bathroom facilities were available but required an additional payment. Understanding the necessity, I availed myself of the facility and finally managed to refresh myself.

The next morning, a host representative came to my room, introduced herself, and invited me to accompany her to the Physiotherapy Training Centre. Upon arrival, I was warmly introduced to the staff and students. The centre stood out as an inclusive training institute, where visually impaired and sighted students, both male and female, trained together in physiotherapy—a truly unique concept.

During my visit, I was introduced as an Indian Blind Physiotherapist, which piqued their curiosity. They asked numerous questions about yoga, pranayama, acupressure, and related practices. I shared insights as best as I could, while closely observing their activities. The inclusive setup and training methods inspired me to consider how such a model could be adapted to Indian conditions.

In the evening, Ms. Inga visited once again and took me to her brother-in-law's family. He had formerly served as the German Ambassador to Egypt. The couple warmly welcomed me, and we enjoyed a lively and engaging conversation on various political and social issues of mutual interest.

As both were fluent in English, it was a pleasure to share thoughts with them. During our discussion, I recounted the recent Bangladesh war with Pakistan. They admired Smt. Indira Gandhi's courage and decisive leadership in taking a bold stance against Pakistan, resulting in the creation of Bangladesh as a new nation.

I Can't Find My Sock!

The next morning, I was scheduled to board a flight from Frankfurt airport to Berlin. However, until the evening, I had not received any information about my transportation or escort. As a result, I requested Ms. Inga to accompany me to Frankfurt, and she kindly agreed to assist me, ensuring I made it to the airport and boarded my flight.

I landed at West Berlin Airport, where Mr. Deshpande, a staff member of the Indian Embassy, was there to attend to me. The Indian Embassy in London had been incredibly helpful in ensuring smooth communication and providing necessary support throughout my journey, especially between London and East Berlin. After a brief introduction, Shri. Deshpande escorted me to the railway station. We traveled a few kilometers, crossed the checkpoint, and finally entered East Berlin City. Dr. Tilash and Mrs. Tilash, the organizers of the International Conference on Placement of the Blind, were eagerly awaiting my arrival.

We had to catch a flight the same evening to Cairo on our way back to India. With only two hours at our disposal for discussions and logistics, I had not eaten until that point. Dr. Tilash managed to arrange some noodles, bread, and butter for me and informed me that we needed to rush to the airport within half an hour. I quickly finished my snack and joined them to head to the airport. Upon arrival, all the other delegates were eagerly waiting for me. About an hour later, we flew to Cairo and reached within three hours. There was no direct flight to Bombay, so we had to take a halt for the night at a hotel. Exhausted from the journey, we enjoyed a much-needed, restful sleep.

We had to check out early in the morning and were getting ready to leave our room, but I couldn't find my second sock! I managed to find one, but the other was nowhere in reach. Repeated announcements urged us to come downstairs, and I was troubled about how to move without matching socks. In a moment of desperation, I pressed all the buttons on the door for help. Two or three attendants arrived and began searching for it. Communication became difficult, so I held up the sock I had and asked them to find the other one. Thankfully, one of the attendants located it and handed it to me. Only then was I able to head downstairs and take the transport. After about an hour, we left for Bombay.

***

Chapter 13

My 2nd Foreign Trip!

"Move out of your comfort zone. You can only grow if you are willing to feel awkward and uncomfortable when you try something new."

- Brian Tracy

Rotary International Scholarship

By 1974-75, my efforts in the rehabilitation of the visually impaired were steadily gaining recognition, not just in Madhya Pradesh but also at the national level. Around this time, an interesting opportunity came my way through an advertisement inviting applications for Rotary International Educational Award. This prestigious award sought to honor individuals who had made significant contributions to society's well-being. Intrigued by it, I applied.

I was delighted to learn that my application got cleared for round 1 at the local level. Following this, I was invited to appear before the selection committee of the District Rotary Club in Valsad for the final round. To my surprise, there were 150 candidates competing for this prestigious scholarship. But eventually my name was announced as the recipient! It was an overwhelming moment of joy and pride. Competing against 150 other candidates, all without any disabilities, made the achievement even more significant. It was a testament to my perseverance and commitment to societal well-being.

This Rotary International Education Award granted me a scholarship to study in the US, propelling me further in my mission to make a difference!

Getting NOC from the Central Government

Studying in the US wasn't an easy endeavour. During that time, a national emergency had been imposed, restricting government employees from traveling abroad. As a State Government employee, I had to get a special permission from the Government of India—a challenging process, to say the least. I made four trips to New Delhi, approaching numerous authorities across various departments to secure a 'No Objection Certificate' (NOC). After considerable effort, I finally obtained the same. However, my hurdles didn't end there. I had to wait for the State Government's approval and also apply for a ten-month leave from my department, which raised eyebrows.

For a middle-class individual, planning an overseas visit was a Herculean task. Securing a No Objection Certificate (NOC) from the Central Government, obtaining permission for extended leave from the State Government, acquiring a passport and visa, arranging appropriate clothing for moderate living, and managing finances were significant challenges. Above all, leaving my family behind was a deeply emotional hurdle. While these efforts demanded determination from anyone, for someone visually impaired like me, the process was even more strenuous and demanding.

Purchasing a Flight Ticket

Next hurdle was purchasing a fight ticket. The Rotary International Club had provided a certain amount for this purpose, but it was insufficient. I needed to contribute an additional ₹4,500, which, though not a huge amount, was beyond my means at the time. I couldn't manage to borrow the sum from relatives or friends, which left me deeply worried.

One morning, on a sudden impulse, I went to the State Bank of India, Residency Branch, and met the Branch Manager, Shri. Rustamji Bhelpuriwala. I explained my situation, the Rotary International Educational Award I had received, and the financial difficulty in purchasing the flight ticket. Being a Rotarian himself, I hoped he might assist me using his discretion. Shri. Bhelpuriwala, a member of the Parsi community—renowned for their generosity and support for noble causes—listened carefully.

After a brief moment of thought, he called his staff, explained my predicament, and directed them to help me open a savings account. He then approved the required amount as a personal loan and deposited it directly into my account. His timely assistance deeply moved me, and I expressed my heartfelt gratitude. I assured him I would repay the loan within three months without delay.

Thanks to Shri. Bhelpuriwala's support, I was finally able to purchase my flight ticket, a crucial step in making my dream a reality.

Finding a Training Institute

Next, I needed to identify a suitable agency in the USA that could provide rehabilitation training at the desired level. This required extensive correspondence, which wouldn't have been possible without the generous support of Shri. Vasant Sangle. A senior citizen retired from the postal services, Shri. Sangle was not only philanthropic but also deeply committed to helping others. Both he and his brother had dedicated years of service to the postal department and were actively involved in the postal union, serving with utmost dedication.

After reaching out to several organizations in the USA, I eagerly awaited a positive response. One morning, I received a letter from the American Foundation for the Blind (AFB), advising me to contact Arkansas Enterprises for the Blind, located in Little Rock, USA. According to AFB, this organization was well-equipped to meet my training needs.

In response to my inquiry, Arkansas Enterprises for the Blind sent me a detailed prospectus outlining their training programs for professionals. The content of the prospectus aligned perfectly with my requirements, making it an ideal choice. I finalized my admission with them, leveraging the scholarship received with Rotary International Education Award.

Finding My Temporary Replacement

Next crucial task was finding an experienced individual to manage the organization's affairs during my absence. After careful consideration, I appointed Shri. N. L. Sharma as the Executive Officer. A long-standing member of the Lions Club, Shri. Sharma brought extensive administrative experience and a strong command of both English and Hindi. His expertise promised significant contributions to enhancing communication, decision-making, and overall organizational behavior.

With Shri. Sharma at the helm, I felt a sense of relief knowing the organization—and particularly its staff—would be in capable hands. His presence would not only ensure smooth operations but also foster improvements in writing skills and fundamental human qualities among the team.

Relocating My Family

Last but not the least, I had to relocate my wife and my little daughter to Nagpur with my in-laws, who graciously agreed to take care of them during my year-long absence.

Finally, on September 6, 1976, I took off for America to embark on my study trip!

Rehabilitation Training Begins

After a journey of nearly 24 hours, I arrived at Little Rock Airport from Mumbai at around 11:00 p.m. A staff member from the Arkansas Enterprises for the Blind was there to receive me. After a brief introduction, we headed to the institution.

The next morning, the supervisor on duty came to escort me to the dining room for breakfast. Later, I was introduced to the Executive Director, Mr. Roy Kumte. He welcomed me warmly and ensured I felt at ease as we discussed the communication and planning required for my studies.

Mr. Kumte, a senior professional with a deep interest in international training, showed a keen understanding of the unique needs of professionals working in different contexts. He specifically inquired about my general needs and any special requirements to address the conditions in India.

Given my focus on the rehabilitation of the visually impaired, my training was structured into three phases, each lasting three months. The program covered rehabilitation teaching, counseling, and blind welfare administration. My first phase involved attending classes that explored various aspects of rehabilitation teaching, laying a solid foundation for the rest of my training.

Mrs. Bally Elder, the Head of the Department of Rehabilitation Teaching, designed a comprehensive training program tailored to my needs. The program focused on the following key areas:

a) Braille writing
b) Typing
c) Alpha communication techniques
d) Vocational evaluation
e) Orientation and Mobility

This well-rounded curriculum set the stage for me to deepen my expertise in rehabilitation teaching and better serve the visually impaired community.

Accordingly, some staff members joined me and introduced me to my respective trainers. I was also introduced to the other international professional trainees studying there. Trainees from Mexico, Chile, Taiwan, and Nigeria were enrolled in similar training programs.

The very next day, my training commenced regularly, following the schedule prepared by Mrs. Elder. She often made unannounced visits to observe trainees during their sessions, ensuring they were following the program as planned.

Typing

From day one itself, I took a particular interest in typing, Braille, and mobility training. Within just three weeks, I had developed my typing skills to a reasonable level, allowing me to type my own letters correctly. At the end of the third month, I typed a letter on my own to Shri. Rustamji Bhelpuriwala, expressing my heartfelt gratitude for the loan he had extended to me, to purchase my flight ticket. By that time, I had fully repaid the loan amount to the bank. Writing this letter was my way of acknowledging his kindness and demonstrating a gesture of goodwill. Shri. Bhelpuriwala responded with great appreciation. He not only acknowledged my letter warmly but also shared it with his staff, remarking, “Training makes a man perfect even without eyesight!”

Although I took pride in my progress with typing, a sense of worry quietly brewed within me—I had not received any news from my family, particularly my daughter. Despite my focus on training and day-to-day activities, her health and well-being were always on my mind, and the silence from home only deepened my anxiety. I was constantly worried about her health. She was just six years old and suffering from primary complex, undergoing regular treatment. I had kept her in Nagpur with her mother and in-laws, where her grandfather ensured meticulous care for her medicines, health check-ups, and nutrition. However no communication from their end filled me with anxiety. Concerned, I approached the Executive Director one morning and shared my worry. Understanding my situation, he kindly allowed me to make a long-distance call to Nagpur that night. It was through this call that I managed to connect with my brother-in-law and gain some reassurance.

One evening, overwhelmed with longing, I decided to write a letter to my daughter. I typed it in English, unsure whether she would be able to read it, but I poured all my emotions and affection into that letter, tears streaming down as I wrote. It was a heartfelt expression of love that I could scarcely put into words otherwise. To my surprise and delight, she replied within a fortnight! Her response brought me immense joy and renewed my longing to return to her. It felt as though her letter had given me wings, lifting my spirits and carrying me closer to my beloved daughter.

Having got sufficiently trained in typing, it was time to move to the next phase.

Mobility

The institution had six mobility instructors, each responsible for training six trainees daily. I was pleasantly surprised to see the emphasis placed on orientation and mobility training in the USA. It was remarkable to learn that this specialized training was considered so vital that several universities offered mobility as a subject at the postgraduate level.

In the USA, mobility was regarded as a critical component of rehabilitation services, highlighting its importance in empowering individuals with visual impairments to navigate their surroundings independently and confidently.

I began reflecting on the state of rehabilitation services for the blind in India, particularly the lack of specialized trainers for mobility training. In most institutions at the time, mobility training was an emerging but largely overlooked aspect of rehabilitation. Despite being an essential component of rehabilitation services, very few organizations working with the blind in India provided training in mobility.

Even today, orientation and mobility training remain absent from the curriculum of many schools and training centers for the blind in India. My entire training program in the USA was tailored to my needs, equipping me with the knowledge and skills to develop a rehabilitation training program that could address these gaps back home.

My mobility instructor had connections with some Indian students and people at the university. She would often greet me with a warm "Namaste," reflecting her familiarity with Indian culture. Curious and eager to connect, I asked her to introduce me to them.

Over time, I became acquainted with several Indian friends. We would occasionally meet, sharing experiences and forming bonds that brought a sense of home away from home. Sometimes, they invited me to their homes for dinner, creating moments of warmth and camaraderie that made my journey even more special.

During mobility training, we used long metal canes, which were an integral part of the process. Initially, my mobility instructor focused on orienting me for indoor mobility, as the institution spanned three to four buildings across a vast campus.

One day, she left me to practice indoor mobility independently, confident in my progress. As I moved around with determination, I unexpectedly collided with a thorny bush and fell. While I took the incident lightly, my instructor was understandably anxious, given her responsibility for a foreign professional trainee. Her concern was genuine and reflected her dedication to ensuring my safety.

From that day onward, she never left me alone during training. She remained by my side, guiding me through orientation and mobility training for the initial three months.

Having being trained in Mobility, it was time for the next phase.

Counselling

Mrs. Pays, my rehabilitation counselor, specialized in counseling at the postgraduate level and had extensive experience in addressing the challenges that arise during counseling. Counseling is a vital discipline in rehabilitation services, as it equips professionals to assess individual needs and work on the development of behavior, attitude, and skills. Goal planning, driven by result-oriented activities, is always the ultimate objective in any rehabilitation case. Counselors, and consequently trainees, acquire qualifications in clinical psychology, behavioral modification, and other allied disciplines.

I found my training in counseling to be far more fulfilling than anything else. Given my deep commitment to serving the cause of the blind, it was essential for me to gain the knowledge needed to address the complex socio-economic and educational challenges that individuals face in India.

During this period, the focus of my training was "Methods and Techniques of Counseling." I received orientation in verbal intelligence tests commonly used for adult clients, and learned about various queries that arise in counseling. One technique that resonated deeply with me was "Reality Therapy," which is particularly effective when dealing with clients who harbor negative attitudes toward individuals or society. This approach proved invaluable in helping me regulate my mind and interact with people of diverse behaviors, attitudes, and skills.

I continue to use this knowledge in my everyday life, as well as in helping others upgrade their skills and navigate their personal challenges.

Additional Classes at University of Arkansas

Since the counseling training required a period of six months, I was advised to attend additional classes at the University of Arkansas. Dr. Dickerson, the head of the department, took special care of overseas professionals receiving training at Arkansas Enterprises for the Blind. The university campus was five kilometers away from the institution, and I had to attend the classes independently. At times, someone would escort me to the campus, but this was not always guaranteed.

I explained my situation to the Executive Director, asking if an escort could be arranged. He responded by suggesting that my mobility instructor should train me to be independent enough to attend the university classes on my own. Unfortunately, my first mobility instructor was not confident that I could handle the independence required for this task. As a result, the Executive Director assigned this responsibility to a Nigerian woman professional, who was completing her postgraduate studies in mobility at the University of Little Rock.

She accepted the task and created a training program for me. As part of this, she dictated my mobility project in Braille and asked me to memorize it within a day or two. With this preparation, I began field training, traveling from Fair Path to the University Campus. My route included walking for about five minutes along the pavement to catch the city bus, which would take me toward the university. I then had to disembark at the designated stop and cross three streets to reach the university.

It took two to three days for me to get familiar with the route and navigate the large campus to find my classroom. During training, one of the challenges was the fear of stepping in front of moving vehicles while crossing the streets. Occasionally, some university students would offer to help me cross, but I always declined, saying, "No, thank you, I am on training."

Once I gained confidence, I was allowed to travel to the university alone. I did well that day, reaching the university gate safely. Unbeknownst to me, my mobility instructor had been observing me from a distance! As soon as I reached the main gate, she rushed over, patted me on the shoulder, and praised me for my success. From that point on, I attended my classes independently. On the way back, however, someone would always offer me a ride back to the institution.

I successfully completed the short-term certificate training at the university, which significantly improved my skills in assessing client needs and developing specific goal plans to assist them.

Administration

After completing my training in counseling, I transitioned to administrative exposure to familiarize myself with the office operations. Mr. Gimy Cordile, the Assistant Director, guided me through the comprehensive workings of the institution. The institution's expenses were primarily funded by the Lions Club, with additional support from the Federal Government allocated to specific areas. It also had its own income-generating activities to sustain its operations.

The institution provided free lunch and breakfast to all staff members, a thoughtful initiative that contributed to employee welfare. Most of the staff were professionally trained for their roles, ensuring efficiency in service delivery. However, whenever a staff member received an opportunity for a better job elsewhere, they often chose to leave. This recurring issue posed a continual challenge for the administration, as it required efforts to maintain the smooth functioning of the institution's established activities despite staff turnover.

Having completed comprehensive training in typing, mobility, counseling, and administration over ten transformative months, my time in the United States was drawing to a close. It was time to return home.

However, before returning to India, I wanted to make use of this opportunity of being there to visit well known organizations who were working for the welfare of the blind. Determined to expand my exposure, I meticulously planned a tour that would take me through various cities in America!

My Tour Begins!

Organizing this tour was no small task. I needed to finalize lodging, boarding, and local transport arrangements for each city. This required extensive planning and correspondence with various agencies to secure the necessary support. Fortunately, institutions and kind hearted souls came forward to assist me to make my tour comfortable.

I decided to begin my tour right from the state of Arkansas, where I had just completed my training in its capital city, Little Rock.

First I decided to pay a visit to 'Goodwill Industries', a remarkable non-profit organization dedicated to empowering people with disabilities. They collected unserviceable items from families, companies, banks, and other commercial establishments, sorted them out, and renewed them. Disabled individuals were engaged throughout the entire process. Once the items were renewed, they were sold at their counters and in sales exhibitions to support the institution's expenses, making their operations self-sustaining. I felt that such initiatives could be adopted in India as well, turning them into income-generating programs for people with disabilities through the medium of our organization (MPWAB).

I also had the opportunity to visit the Arkansas School for the Blind, one of the most advanced institutions of its kind in the USA. The school had a significant number of children who were both deaf and blind, and they were taught with the help of hearing aids. Special teachers for the deaf-blind were assigned to meet their educational needs. The school even had a swimming pool, and the children were encouraged to learn and enjoy swimming during their leisure time.

During my visit, the Superintendent of the school shared an interesting anecdote: Shri. Ved Mehta, the renowned English writer, had studied there for a few years! He then continued his education in the United States, pursuing a post-graduate degree in English at Oxford University, UK. He eventually settled in the United States, where he became a journalist and columnist in New York. His books, 'Face to Face' and 'Walking on Indian Streets', became widely popular.

Thus, after visiting those remarkable institutions, it was time for me to bid farewell to Little Rock—a city that had given me invaluable rehabilitation training and an unforgettable experience.

As I prepared to leave, I reflected on the ten months I had spent there. It was a period of immense learning, forging friendships with professionals from various countries, and gaining insights into the American lifestyle. These experiences not only enriched my understanding but also empowered me with the confidence and vision to work for the cause of rehabilitation in the years ahead.

With a heart full of gratitude and determination, I left Little Rock and embarked on the next leg of my journey—heading to Chicago!

Chicago

Dr. Shashi Das from Indore, who was working in Chicago, graciously volunteered to host me during my stay in the city. His willingness to help made my visit to Chicago more comfortable and enjoyable. He receivedmeattheAirportandwasmyhostfor3days.He not only availed three days leave but also escorted me to visit various institutions!

First, I visited Hadley School for the Blind, which was extending its services at International level to visually handicapped people. They conduct correspondence courses on several subjects, enabling blind youths to achieved desirable command on the subject they prefer. Dr. Richard Kenny, was a deaf-blind professional, holding the position of Director of the Institution.

Being on educational tour under Rotary International Education Award, I was equally interested to visit their Headquarters. Concerned officials received us with utmost cordiality and expressed their happiness towards this visit. I apprised them with the training I availed with their scholarship and how I would be putting all this training to good use upon my return to India.

I also visited Lion International Headquarters and apprised them that I had completed ten months training at Arkansas Enterprises for the Blind at Little rock. Thus, officers at the headquarters were happy to know that overseas professionals, like me, were availing desired training to enhance their professional skills in the larger interest of human development. Lastly, I visited Lion workshop where sheltered employments were provided to those blind youths, who were not in a position to stand in open market.

At the end of my visit to Chicago, I headed to Louisville.

Louisville

Upon my arrival at the Louisville Airport, I was warmly received by representatives from the Lions Club. They escorted me to their facility.

Without wasting a moment, I headed straight to the telephone and asked the operator to provide me with the contact number of any Indian person in the area. However, the operator politely declined, explaining that it was not possible to provide numbers without a specific name. I tried to reason with him, sharing my situation as a blind person from India and expressing my wish to connect with fellow Indians to make my extended stay more comforting. Despite my earnest plea, the operator was unable to assist.

Not willing to give up, I made another attempt. I requested the operator to provide me with the contact number of the Indian Chamber of Commerce. I figured this might be a way to establish a connection with someone from the local Indian community.

Thankfully, this approach worked. Through the Chamber of Commerce, I managed to get the information I needed. After a few calls and some persistent efforts, I finally got in touch with Professor Kulkarni, a fellow Indian originally from Poona.

Speaking to him brought a sense of relief and joy. The conversation was a much-needed bridge to my homeland, providing comfort and a sense of belonging amidst unfamiliar surroundings. It also set the tone for my stay in Louisville, ensuring that I had some support and connection during my time there.

Mr. Kulkarni's hospitality was truly heartwarming. He came to pick me up at 6 PM, and without hesitation, insisted that I stay with his family for the long weekend. His kindness immediately made me feel at home. We drove to his residence, where he introduced me to his wife and son. The warmth of their welcome was a true reflection of Indian hospitality, even far from home.

That night, there was a get-together organized by Indian university students. Mr. Kulkarni and I joined them, and we enjoyed their cultural program, which was followed by a delicious dinner. The atmosphere was lively, and it felt great to connect with fellow countrymen, even in such a distant land.

The following day, by coincidence, there was a Satyanarayan Puja at a family's home. It was a wonderful occasion for all the Indians in the community to gather. After the Puja, we enjoyed a hearty lunch together, surrounded by friends and fellow countrymen.

Later Dr. Kulkarni kindly accompanied me for shopping. I bought a suit, safari cloth, and some dresses for my daughter, along with a few other items.

Throughout the weekend, Dr. Kulkarni and his wife went out of their way to ensure my comfort. They made me feel like part of their family.

On Monday, while offices and institutions resumed their regular activities, I had the opportunity to visit the Rehabilitation Centre and the American Braille Printing House, two prominent institutions that greatly influenced my perspective on rehabilitation for the blind. Dr. Kulkarni, being busy with his work, could not join me that day. However, Mrs. Kulkarni kindly accompanied me to these two institutions.

The Rehabilitation Centre was impressive, providing a wide range of need-based services to individuals. Individual counseling played a significant role, allowing clients to engage in goal planning that was tailored to their unique attitudes and aptitudes. The focus was on empowering the clients to take charge of their progress and development. The centre also collaborated with other agencies to ensure that clients received comprehensive services. For those with low vision, low vision therapists worked with them to help utilize their remaining vision to the fullest. This was achieved through proper devices, training, and continuous follow-up services.

The American Braille Printing House, on the other hand, was a remarkable institution. It transcribed an array of books into Braille, making knowledge and literature accessible to the blind. The press supplied Braille books to the National Library of Congress, which, through its extensive network, ensured that these books were distributed to blind individuals across the country. This initiative truly highlighted the efforts being made to ensure that the visually impaired had equal access to education and information.

Having done with my tour in Louisville, I headed towards Washington.

Washington

At the Washington airport, I was received by Mr. Shirodkar, a staff member of the Indian Embassy. Our first stop was the Embassy, where I was introduced to many of the staff members. Afterward, we made our way to Mr. Shirodkar's residence, where I was to stay during my visit. His wife was away in India for a few weeks, so he was managing the household on his own, but he was more than happy to host me.

The following day, Dr. Paul, the Public Relations Officer at the Embassy, joined me for a series of visits to various institutions. These had been meticulously planned in advance, with proper coordination with the embassy authorities. The visits offered me an opportunity to explore more about the rehabilitation programs and services for the visually impaired in Washington, further enriching my understanding and experience.

Our first stop was the Department of Rehabilitation of the Federal Government, where we engaged in a detailed discussion with an officer about the programs and services they offered for individuals with disabilities in the United States. During this briefing, I learned about several important legislations enacted to support the socio-economic rehabilitation of blind people across the country. Notably, social security coverage was universally available, ensuring that every individual, including those unable to earn their livelihood, had their basic needs met. This system underscored the nation's commitment to inclusivity and welfare.

Next, we visited the National Library of Congress, which housed an impressive collection of Braille books and large-print materials designed for individuals with low vision. The library's services were backed by legislation that obligated the government to provide accessible materials for blind individuals.

I also had the opportunity to visit a dedicated radio station that focused on fostering spiritual awareness and providing relevant information for blind individuals. The station designed and broadcast programs tailored specifically to the interests and needs of the blind community, ensuring they stayed informed and engaged on par with the general public. I was informed that similar radio stations operated in a network across various cities in the United States, demonstrating a well-organized effort to uplift and connect the blind community through accessible media.

On the final day of my stay in Washington, I was invited for dinner by a kind lady who was a staff member of the Indian Embassy. She lived quite far from the embassy, but despite the distance, Mr. Shirodkar graciously accompanied me to her residence. The evening was delightful, steeped in a warm and familiar Indian atmosphere that made me feel right at home. We enjoyed engaging conversations and a meal reminiscent of home, which left me deeply touched.

My visit to Washington proved to be incredibly resourceful and enriching. I remain deeply grateful to the Indian Embassy, its staff members, and especially Mr. Shirodkar, who went to great lengths to ensure my visit was meaningful and comfortable.

With that, it was time to bid farewell to Washington and embark on the next leg of my journey—to New York.

New York

In New York, my accommodation was arranged at the Institute of Independent Living, an institution primarily dedicated to serving aging blind individuals. However, it also extended rehabilitation services to others on a short-term basis, catering to specific needs as required.

During my stay, I had the privilege of receiving extensive support from Mr. Robert Jackal, the Director of the Helen Keller International Institute. His assistance proved invaluable in facilitating visits to various institutions in and around New York. Mr. Jackal had previously worked in India as a professional consultant specializing in mobility, and many of us in the field were already acquainted with him.

On the very first day in New York, Mr. Robert Jackal accompanied me to two significant institutions: the American Foundation for the Blind and Helen Keller International. The latter, known in its earlier years as the American Foundation for the Overseas Blind, held a storied history of providing critical services in the field of orientation and mobility. For several years, its headquarters were based in Kuala Lumpur, focusing on manpower development and support across various Asian countries.

Mr. Jackal's contributions to the cause were deeply rooted in his extensive experience. He had initially worked with the American Foundation for the Overseas Blind and later contributed his expertise to the Christoffel-Blindenmission (CBM) in India.

I then visited 'Lighthouse for the Blind' which proved to be exceptionally inspiring and showcased a model worth replicating globally. The institution's innovative approach catered to blind infants and young children, who attended the center daily under the guidance of professionally trained teachers. These educators were dedicated to skill development, ensuring that the blind children achieved capabilities on par with sighted children of their age.

One remarkable aspect of their program was its integration with a nearby nursery for sighted children. After the lunch hour, the blind infants and kids would join their sighted peers in the nursery, promoting inclusivity and mutual understanding. This ground-breaking approach created a two-way benefit: it helped the blind children adapt to a more integrated environment while also sensitizing the sighted children to diversity and fostering empathy from a young age.

Last but not the least, I visited the renowned Guide Dog School at Morris Town, where I spent an entire day immersed in understanding their comprehensive training program for guide dogs. The process of preparing these dogs to serve as dependable companions and navigators for blind individuals was nothing short of extraordinary. I was even given the unique opportunity to experience walking through the city with a guide dog. The dog adeptly guided me to various places, including a laundry, restaurant, and grocery shop, demonstrating exceptional obedience and skill by crossing streets only when the traffic light turned green.

The training of both the guide dogs and their prospective masters involved a meticulous series of procedures and phases. Before a guide dog was assigned to a blind individual, candidates were thoroughly assessed and registered with the school. Factors like age, height, and mobility level were carefully evaluated, along with the client's specific needs and behavioural tendencies. Similarly, the selection of a guide dog for a particular person depended on the dog's temperament, height, movement level, and intelligence to ensure the perfect match for the user's requirements.

Witnessing the entire process of training and pairing the guide dogs with their prospective users left a deep impression on me. The dedication, patience, and attention to detail shown by the trainers to ensure that blind individuals could lead more independent lives were truly commendable. The commitment of everyone involved in this noble mission was inspiring, and their efforts deserved the highest praise for making such a meaningful impact on the lives of the blind in their country.

In this manner, my 12-day tour across various cities in the United States came to a successful conclusion. Each stop enriched me with new experiences, invaluable insights, and cherished connections that I would treasure for a lifetime. From exploring pioneering institutions to meeting compassionate individuals, every moment contributed to my understanding of rehabilitation and empowerment for the visually impaired.

It was time for me to bid farewell to the United States, but before returning to India, there was one more wish I hoped to fulfill – to visit Paris!

Paris!

In Paris, my heart was set on paying homage to Louis Braille, the pioneer who revolutionized education for the blind. I was determined to visit Coupvray, his birthplace, but I didn't know anyone in Paris who could guide me there. Dr. R. T. Vyas from NAB India, understanding my wish, reached out to the Chairman of the World Council for Blind Welfare of the Blind (WCWB), headquartered in Paris, to assist me. The WCWB graciously arranged for an escort to accompany me on this meaningful journey.

When I arrived in Paris, the escort was there to receive me at the airport, and we set off for Coupvray. It was a Saturday, and most establishments were closed, yet this special gesture, offering me an escort on a holiday, felt like a privilege.

The journey to Coupvray, over 40 kilometers away from Paris, was an emotional one. We traveled by train, as there were no road transport facilities to reach the small village. Upon arriving at the humble house of Louis Braille, I was overwhelmed with emotion and respect. This was the birthplace of the man who had brought light to the lives of millions of blind individuals around the world through his invention of the Braille script.

Inside the house, I found a statue of Louis Braille, surrounded by his personal belongings and items on display. To me, this place felt more like a temple, a sacred space honoring the immense contribution he made to the blind community. I stood there in silence for a long while, paying my respects to the great man whose vision helped break the barriers of ignorance and opened the doors to knowledge for those without sight.

With my overseas journey now complete, I boarded the flight from Paris and made my way back to Bombay, my beloved home. After ten months of travel, learning, and personal growth, I finally returned to India, carrying with me a wealth of knowledge and experiences that would prove invaluable in the years ahead.

The exposure I gained during this time—spanning various fields, understanding the intricacies of communication, and deepening my knowledge of the subject—was beyond measure. All of this would play a vital role in furthering the cause I had taken up in Madhya Pradesh.

American Lifestyle

After returning to India, I finally had the opportunity to relax and reflect on my experiences in America. People around me were eager to hear about the training I underwent, the American lifestyle, and everything I observed during my ten-month journey.

To share my experiences, MPWAB organized a meeting and invited Dr. Thomas, the Principal of Indore School of Social Work, to chair the event. The gathering included an enthusiastic audience keen to learn about my time in the USA.

During the first half of the session, I detailed the training I received in rehabilitation services, discussing the methodologies, institutions, and insights I had gained. In the second half, the audience's curiosity shifted to the American lifestyle and values, which I narrated as follows.

America, being a developed nation, had a robust social security system that ensured every individual was covered. While this system offered a safety net, it also had its drawbacks, especially when it came to the community's work ethic. From my observations, I noticed that many unemployed individuals didn't make a significant effort to find jobs. In the institution where I was staying, a significant number of people—some married, others single, and even those over 35—were unemployed and surviving solely on social security benefits. Why bother looking for work when the system provides for their basic needs?

This reliance on social security, in my view, was not a healthy sign for the community. It fostered a sense of complacency rather than self-sufficiency and personal growth.

I had an interesting conversation with an aging couple, whose perspectives on American and Indian lifestyles were thought-provoking. The husband was blind, and his wife was sighted. Despite their disabilities, they managed to maintain a car and a good standard of living, relying entirely on their social security benefits. However, what struck me as concerning was that they lived alone, while their daughter-in-law volunteered at an old age home. This raised questions about the level of responsibility and sensitivity towards aging parents in American society. On one hand, people in the community were willing to volunteer their services for others in need, yet, on the other hand, there seemed to be a lack of responsibility towards caring for one's own elderly family members. It was a contradictory attitude that highlighted a gap in societal values.

I encountered another aging couple who, much like the first, lived alone. The husband was blind, and his wife was sighted. Their daughter, around 17 or 18 years old, lived elsewhere and only visited occasionally to comfort her parents. This situation struck me as particularly unusual, so I asked them directly, "Why isn't your daughter staying with you?"

The couple's response was revealing: "We Americans do not like young people to depend on their parents once they are able to earn." This response gave me a glimpse into the cultural values in America—values that emphasized independence, even at the expense of familial bonds.

The Executive Director of Arkansas Enterprises once asked me, "When the cow is considered a sacred animal in India, why do they roam the streets and disturb traffic?" My answer couldn't fully satisfy him. He believed that if cows are sacred, they should be cared for properly by their owners, and not allowed to roam freely on the streets.

Young boys and girls in America often develop relationships, sometimes leading to courtship and eventual decisions about becoming life partners. I recall an example of courtship between two university students. The boy assured the girl that they would marry after completing their studies. However, after some time, the boy refused to marry her. One morning, the girl came to the university campus with a revolver and shot him dead. Sadly, such incidents are not uncommon in American society.

Americans are highly vigilant about their human rights and actively take action to uphold them. One of the distinctive characteristics of American society is the formation of associations or organizations with common positive objectives. Blind people, in particular, have strong, active organizations that take assertive action. These groups often pursue their rights by lobbying congressional representatives and organizing in large numbers until specific legislation is enacted in their favour.

It took more than an hour to share my experiences with the audience. Chief Guest, Dr. Thomas, in his address appreciated my venture acquiring special higher education in USA and the experience gained during my stay over there.

***

Chapter 14

National Association for the Blind (MP Branch)

"When we do the best that we can, we never know what miracle is wrought in our life, or in the life of another."

-Hellen Keller

In June 1976, the Emergency in India was withdrawn. Following the Lok Sabha elections, the Janata Party emerged victorious, and Shri. Morarji Desai assumed office as the Prime Minister of India. Under his leadership, from 1977 onwards, the government steered the country in a new direction.

The philosophy of Shri. Jayaprakash Narayan gained prominence during this period, advocating for a total revolution—a transformative political approach aimed at empowering people at the grassroots level. National development programs began prioritizing services for the unreached, ensuring greater inclusivity in governance and welfare initiatives.

Meeting Mr. Henry Viscardi !

The National Society for Equal Opportunity for the Handicapped organized a national conference at Birla House, Bombay, with the theme "The Total Revolution of Society." The conference was inaugurated by Prime Minister Shri. Morarji Desai. As a participant, I gained valuable insights into the challenges faced by rural communities, particularly in poverty and illiteracy, and the need for dedicated efforts to address these issues.

Mr. Henry Viscardi, then serving as a Rehabilitation Consultant to the President of the United States, also attended the conference. In his thought-provoking lecture, he emphasized the importance of prioritizing services for the disabled, especially in rural areas.

His work and powerful message served as an inspiration to everyone present at the conference.

Keeping all these aspects in mind, the National Society for Equal Opportunity for the Handicapped organized a national seminar on rural disabled individuals living in challenging conditions near Pune. At that time, I was actively working for the welfare of all categories of disabled people under the banner of 'Apang Kalyan Sangh'. As the President of the organization, I encouraged senior workers from various fields of disability care to participate in the seminar.

During the seminar, the concept of "need-based rehabilitation" gained significant traction as a universal approach. This led to the emergence of community-based rehabilitation programs for rural disabled persons, which became increasingly popular for implementation by Non-Governmental Organizations (NGOs). Eventually, this approach was incorporated into national policy, marking a transformative shift in the rehabilitation landscape.

Establishment of NAB (MP Branch)

Meanwhile, the National Association for the Blind, India (NAB), proposed the establishment of its state branch in Madhya Pradesh. Until then, the MP Welfare Association for the Blind (MPWAB) had been functioning as NAB's state representative. However, circumstances no longer allowed this arrangement to continue.

Thus, in 1979, we formally established the Madhya Pradesh state branch of NAB, bringing together senior workers and office bearers as members of the executive council. Shri. Jagdish Patel from Ahmedabad, a senior NAB representative, attended the meeting as an observer. I was nominated as the General Secretary of the newly formed branch.

For about a year, the NAB MP branch office operated from the premises of MPWAB. During this time, Shri. Jitendra Choksi, a low-vision specialist who had been working with MPWAB as a Development Officer, transitioned to the NAB MP branch in the same role.

Focusing on Rural Blind

With this new responsibility, I was able to dedicate more time to developing need-based programs and innovative projects for meaningful impact. One such initiative was a one-day workshop on the rehabilitation of the rural blind, where we invited Shri. Ajit Jogi, the Collector of Indore, as the Chief Guest.

While introducing the topic, I emphasized the need to establish a rehabilitation center specifically for the rural blind. The goal was to provide them with training in various rural trades, enabling them to engage in agro-based occupations while staying within their families. This approach would discourage migration to cities and help them sustain themselves in familiar surroundings.

Shri. Ajit Jogi appreciated the proposal and inquired about the kind of support required from the district administration. The primary need was a piece of land where activities related to agriculture, horticulture, and cottage industries could be developed, along with space for a hostel to accommodate the beneficiaries.

Project at Dakacha

The Collector was generous enough to identify and allocate a 27-acre piece of land near Dakacha, situated on both sides of the Agra-Bombay Road. This marked a significant step forward in our mission. On March 2, 1983, Shri. Prakash Chandra Sethi, Home Minister of India, laid the foundation stone for the project. It was another milestone in the service of the blind in Madhya Pradesh, and I take great pride in having been the driving force behind its initiation.

Developing the land required extensive efforts. We sought support from the District Administration, the Agricultural Department, and even the Agriculture College to help establish sustainable practices. However, one of the major challenges we faced was the scarcity of water. The groundwater level in the entire area was significantly low, posing a considerable hurdle in making the land productive.

Bhabra Tribal District Project

Our appeal to extend services to the rural blind reached a veteran social worker from the remote village of Bhabhra. He approached us with a proposal to start a school and rehabilitation center in the tribal district of Madhya Pradesh. He assured us that if we could implement the project there, he would offer some land along with a constructed portion of his building to support the initiative.

At his insistence, I visited Bhabhra along with Shri. Ganesh Shaligram Bhatt from Gwalior, a retired faculty member from the Music College. Shri. Bhatt was willing to take on the responsibility of leading the proposed venture. After assessing the feasibility, we decided to start the project in the available space provided by the social worker. Shri. Bhatt and his wife settled in Bhabhra and worked tirelessly to identify blind children from the surrounding villages.

Over time, with support from the district administration, we acquired additional land, allowing us to construct a dedicated hostel and school building. A trained special educator was appointed, enabling blind children to receive an education on par with their sighted peers. Eventually, the time came for these children to transition into mainstream education under the integrated education system.

This was a new concept, and initially, there was strong resistance from local schools and teachers who were unwilling to admit blind students. Despite persistent opposition, we continued advocating for their inclusion. After multiple discussions and appeals to the district education authorities, they finally directed local schools to admit blind children.

With time, these children not only adapted but also excelled, proving their capabilities. Their performance in academics and other activities earned them respect from teachers and fellow students alike, breaking barriers and fostering an environment of inclusion.

***

Chapter 15

1981 - International Year of Disabled People

"Keep your face to the sunshine and you cannot see the shadow."

- Helen Keller

The United Nations designated 1981 as the International Year for Disabled Persons, with the theme: "Protection of Rights, Equalization of Opportunities, and Full Participation for the Disabled." In India, both the government and NGOs working for the disabled embraced this initiative with great enthusiasm, focusing on expanding socio-economic opportunities and securing a rightful place in society for disabled individuals.

One significant outcome of this global effort was the spontaneous involvement of banks, which came forward to provide loans to disabled individuals to help them establish self-employment ventures. Recognizing this opportunity, I took the initiative, in my capacity as President of Apang Kalyan Sangh, to engage a Placement Officer who would actively connect disabled individuals with loan opportunities offered by various banks. This step proved instrumental in turning financial assistance into real, sustainable self-employment projects.

The initiative was highly appreciated, not only by disabled youths who benefited from it but also by society at large. The cooperation extended to banks in clearing loan proposals further strengthened their confidence in supporting such ventures. In recognition of these efforts, the Department of Social Welfare, Government of Madhya Pradesh, honored me with a citation and a cash prize, reinforcing the impact of our work in empowering disabled individuals.

Book Translation

With the momentum gained during the International Year for Disabled Persons, the United Nations extended its commitment by declaring a decade dedicated to spreading broader awareness within the global community. Capt. H. M. Desai, Secretary General, contributed to this initiative by writing a book on the World Programme of Action concerning disabled persons in English. The responsibility of translating this book into Hindi was entrusted to me, with assistance from Dr. Datrange and Shri. Arun Mathur, both from NAB, along with Mrs. Alaknanda Sane.

Translating an international document into Hindi was a new experience for us, offering both challenges and valuable insights into the nuances of language and expression at a global level. The translation progressed steadily in a collaborative and cordial environment, and we successfully completed nearly three-fourths of the work. However, midway through the project, Shri. Arun Mathur had to withdraw due to certain administrative allegations. Despite this setback, we persevered, receiving additional support from Mrs. Alaknanda Sane, and ultimately completed the translation.

After tireless efforts, the book was printed at Nai Dunia Press. The Department of Social Welfare, Government of Madhya Pradesh, provided financial support for its release. This translated work marked a significant milestone—it was the first time that a global vision of human dignity for disabled persons was made available in Hindi. The book became a valuable resource, helping professionals, administrators, and parents of disabled individuals understand their roles and responsibilities in fostering an inclusive society.

Establishing Braille Press at Indore

During the International Year for Disabled Persons, the Commissioner of Indore convened a meeting to strengthen need-based initiatives for disabled individuals. A special representative from UNICEF also participated in the discussions. For some time, we had been planning to establish a state-level Braille Press in Indore. In support of this initiative, the Indore Development Corporation allotted a piece of land for the construction of the Braille Press building.

With this in mind, I raised the issue before the UNICEF representative, requesting assistance in procuring Braille Press equipment for Madhya Pradesh as a necessary contribution to the education of blind children. He accepted the request, and after about a year, the State Government acquired the equipment. However, instead of setting it up in Indore, the government decided to relocate the project to Bilaspur, aligning with the preferences of the Chief Minister and the Social Welfare Minister.

Despite our persistent efforts, we were unable to bring the project to Indore. In response, NAB, MP Branch, took the initiative to construct the Braille Press building in Indore with generous financial support from Shri. Sharad Gardi and grant-in-aid from the Government of India. Given the circumstances, NAB, MP had to procure a smaller Braille Press setup through its own efforts. However, this setup was insufficient to meet the growing demand for transcribing textbooks for primary and secondary education.

***

Chapter 16

Jyotsna and Ajay

"My father didn't tell me how to live. He lived and let me watch him do it."

—Clarence Budington Kelland

My daughter Jyotsna was a science student. Until her graduation, she performed reasonably well in her studies. During her childhood, I was abroad, so she studied in Nagpur with her grandparents. She returned to Indore and joined the sixth standard in an English-medium school. I did not take any special efforts to look after her studies. She completed her graduation, and proper counseling was provided to her at the appropriate time for choosing a career. Her inclination toward a Master's degree in social work was obvious, but the job market leaned toward business management. Thus, she availed herself of the opportunity to pursue a one-year business management diploma as a priority option. After completing the one-year course in business management, she joined a post-graduate program in social work. She performed well in her post-graduation and came out as the outstanding student. She achieved the prestigious "Gandhi Centenary Best Student Award," which was given to the best student of the final year. She worked with NGOs for two years and then joined Help Age India. Later on she moved on to Care India

She was now a grown-up girl, and we had to settle her marriage. Fortunately, we found Shri. Ajay Sarwaikar as a good match for her. He was a post-graduate in Physics, belonging to a reputed, educated family. Moreover, his family was also somewhat acquainted with us. She got married on 12 May 1995 and moved to Bhopal to begin her newly married life. She had been a part and parcel of our lives for 25 years, and it became difficult for us to be without her. For a few weeks, we deeply felt her absence and took some time to adjust to the changing scenario.

Ajay, then went into business himself and over time he transformed into a successful business leader, becoming a magnet in his industry. His remarkable work earned him the opportunity to visit more than 15 Asian and European countries. Jyotsna, too, has now established herself as a Development Professional in the Rural Development Department of the Madhya Pradesh government.

***

Chapter 17

Retirement

"I see retirement as just another of these reinventions, another chance to do new things and be a new version of myself."

-Walt Mossberg

I retired from the M. Y. Government Hospital on 31 December 1991, after availing one year of extension of service. I was fully satisfied with my performance and dedication to the profession during my government assignment. However, my involvement in the social field did not allow me to earn from my profession as a private practitioner. As a result, I was unable to make myself financially sound as I had hoped.

Starting a Diploma Program in MPWAB

To make professional training accessible to visually impaired youth, I played a pivotal role after my retirement in initiating a two-year diploma course in physiotherapy as a key program under the MP Welfare Association for the Blind in Indore. As I write this autobiography, many visually impaired individuals have established themselves as skilled physiotherapists, earning the trust of patients and the respect of their communities.

Among them, Ms. Fatima Jamali, a physiotherapist working at Arihant Hospital in Indore, stands out for her commendable reputation among orthopedic surgeons, patients, and the wider community. I take immense pride in her achievements and hope that every visually impaired youth aspires to follow her example in pursuing their career goals.

My Attempt at Business!

After my retirement, I decided to pursue a viable business opportunity to improve my financial situation. Some well-wishers suggested that I apply for an LPG distributorship from the Ministry of Petroleum on compassionate grounds. To support this endeavor, I reached out to friends and well-wishers, requesting their assistance in leveraging their networks to help me secure the distributorship. I had the opportunity to meet with the then Prime Minister, Shri. Narasimha Rao, and a few other prominent dignitaries regarding the matter. Shri. Sunil Dutt, the renowned film actor and esteemed social worker, graciously recommended my case. As a result, the Prime Minister directed my application to the relevant ministry with favorable remarks. Shri. Satish Sharma, the Minister for Petroleum, kindly approved my application and granted me the LPG distributorship. This was truly a significant achievement, allowing me to establish a meaningful self-employment venture.

However, securing the necessary investment of Rs. 10.00 lakhs for the venture was a significant concern. To make it possible, I mortgaged my own house and managed to secure a loan of Rs. 6.00 lakhs. In the shortest time, I successfully launched the LPG distributorship under the name Kedar Enterprises by March 1994. The business operated smoothly for three years. During this period, my daughter Jyotsna got married, and the management of the distributorship became increasingly challenging. As a result, my son-in-law, Shri. Ajay Sarwaikar, was called upon to assist in overseeing the business operations.

Around this time, there was a severe shortage of LPG gas in Indore, and incidents of gas cylinder thefts became a major concern. On top of this, I faced a financial shortage of working capital to ensure a smooth supply of LPG cylinders to my customers. In response, I was compelled to involve a financier. The Indian Oil Corporation (IOCL) authorities recommended a financier of their choice, who slowly began to interfere in the internal management of the business. While he assured me of a steady supply of cylinders, he also began managing my gas warehouse.

Moreover, he insisted that his wife be made a business partner, which I could not accept. Together, he and his wife, leveraging their influence with the IOCL authorities, began misusing their positions to undermine the reputation of the business. When I refused to make his wife a financial partner, the financier took drastic action—he forcibly removed 380 gas cylinders from my storehouse, which ultimately led to the termination of my distributorship.

I took my case to the higher authorities of IOCL, filing a formal complaint against the officer involved in the malpractice. An inquiry was initiated into the officer's actions, and at the same time, arbitration proceedings were set up to address the dispute. Over the course of twelve years, four different arbitrators handled the case, ultimately delivering only partial justice. As the process dragged on, I lost interest in regaining the distributorship, especially since there was no one available to manage the LPG distributorship business on my behalf. Thus I pulled the plug and shut down my business!

Following the unfortunate events with the gas agency, my daughter Jyotsna and her husband, Shri. Ajay Sarwaikar, were forced to leave Indore under deeply distressing circumstances.

***

Chapter 18

Acknowledgment from the Parliament

"All our dreams can come true if we have the courage to pursue them."

- Walt Disney

The decade from 1991 to 2000 brought significant achievements for disabled people in India. One of the major milestones was the enactment of the Rehabilitation Council of India Act in 1992 by the Parliament. The principles of this Act were aimed at regulating professional services for various categories of disabled people. It focused on the development of manpower in the field, the registration of professional workers, and the monitoring of services provided to the disabled community. This legislation marked a crucial step in the formalization and enhancement of disability services in the country.

Another landmark achievement came with the enactment of 'The Persons with Disabilities (Equal Opportunities, Protection of Rights and Full Participation) Act, 1995,' which came into force on February 7, 1996. This Act mobilized both central and state government machinery to address issues concerning disabled individuals. A Chief Commissioner at the central level and Commissioners at the state level were appointed to resolve the grievances of disabled people.

Under the Act, Braille courses were organized for those working in the field but lacking formal training in the subject. These courses were aimed at enhancing the skills of teachers, professional workers, educators, and ophthalmologists. All professionals in the disability sector were registered with the Rehabilitation Council of India, ensuring that only trained workers could operate in the field.

Initially, I played a key role in organizing Braille courses with senior teachers and other professionals. The Persons with Disabilities Act of 1995 recognized only seven disabilities: Blindness, Low Vision, Hearing Impairment, Orthopedic Conditions, Mental Illness, Mental Retardation, and Leprosy. However, the need for services for other disabilities led to the adoption of the "National Trust Act – 1999," which expanded coverage to include Autism, Cerebral Palsy, Mental Retardation, and Multiple Disabilities.

As a whole, all categories of disabled individuals were covered under the two acts mentioned. However, experience revealed by professionals in the field showed that there were many gaps in the implementation and interpretation of the provisions outlined in these acts. This led to a growing demand for revising both acts, with the aim of making them more conducive, effective, and mandatory for the respective departments responsible for their execution.

***

Chapter 19

Awards & Recognition!

"Aim at the sun, and you may not reach it; but your arrow will fly far higher than if aimed at an object on a level with yourself."

- Joel Hawes

The services we had nurtured and cherished for over past 50 years, came to be recognized and honoured, which brought immense sense of fulfillment.

Recognition from All India Confederation of the Blind

The year 1987 was celebrated across India as the Centennial Year for Organized Services for the Blind. This milestone marked 100 years since Christian Missionary Nun Annie Sharp established the first school for the blind in Amritsar in 1887. The school was later relocated to Dehradun, where it continues to provide commendable services to numerous blind children.

To honor this occasion, the All India Confederation of the Blind organized a grand event in New Delhi. As part of the celebrations, twelve dedicated volunteers who had made significant contributions to the field of blind welfare were recognized and honored with a citation and a silver memento. I was fortunate to be among the recipients of this prestigious award. This recognition not only acknowledged our past efforts but also served as a motivation to continue working for the cause with renewed enthusiasm.

Divan Memorial Award & Rustamji Alpaiwala Award

In recognition of my active involvement in promoting services for all categories of disabled people, the National Society for the Equal Opportunity for Disabled conferred upon me their prestigious Divan Memorial Award in 1992. The National Association for the Blind (NAB) India also honored me with their most prestigious Rustamji Alpaiwala Award in 1993. Social services are always initiated with dedication, often without expectation of any return. However, there are moments when appreciation from society helps recognize such efforts. This recognition, much like a glass of water for a thirsty traveler after a long journey, becomes the nectar needed to continue the mission. I truly experienced that sense of fulfillment when receiving these awards.

Indira Gandhi Samaj Sewa Award

The Madhya Pradesh state government instituted the Indira Gandhi Samaj Sewa Award at the end of the 20th century. These awards, which had been pending for three years, were presented in a grand ceremony in March 2002 for three consecutive years. I was fortunate to receive the award alongside eminent social worker Shri. Subbarao, a follower of Shri. Jayprakash Narayanji, and Smt. Kanta Ben of Mewali. The awards were presented by the Governor of MP, His Excellency Dr. Bhai Mahavir, in the esteemed presence of Chief Minister Shri. Digvijay Singh and Social Welfare Minister Smt. Jamuna Devi.

Institutional National Award (2004) for MPWAB

The Government of India presents an institutional award each year to a select few organizations for their outstanding performance in their respective fields. The long-standing, comprehensive services of MP Welfare Association for the Blind, supported by a dedicated team of workers, public support, and assistance from both state and central governments, made it possible for the organization to be chosen for the Institutional National Award in 2004. It was my privilege to receive this award from His Excellency Dr. APJ Abdul Kalam, the President of India, on December 3, 2004. This long-awaited dream turned into a reality and served as a well-deserved consolation for all of us who had dedicated ourselves to the organization over the years. This prestigious recognition was a testament to the tireless and devoted work we had put in to support the visually impaired community in Madhya Pradesh and brought MP Welfare Association for the Blind onto the national stage.

Cavin Kare Ability Foundation Award

The Ability Foundation, Chennai, instituted an award exclusively for disabled individuals who have made significant contributions in their field. This award is given to those whose services have been widely recognized at the national level. The foundation invites applications from across the country, and out of 300 applications, 16 are shortlisted for final consideration. I was fortunate to be selected for this prestigious Ability Foundation Award, which was conferred upon me during a grand ceremony held at Pragati Maidan, Delhi, on February 23, 2008.

IBN7-SuperIdol Award

The IBN Award was established by a group of renowned philanthropic organizations, including IBN7 News Channel,

Bhaskar Newspaper, Bajaj Insurance, Being Human Trust (headed by Salman Khan), and several others. This award was conferred upon thirteen individuals with disabilities from various categories, all of whom, despite their challenges, became models not only for their respective categories but also for society as a whole. Actor Salman Khan presented the award to the recipients at the Taj End Hotel on November 23, 2012. It was a moment of great satisfaction for me and a meaningful recognition of the services I had dedicated over the past 50 years for the cause of the blind and individuals with associated disabilities.

***

Chapter 20

Services for People with "Low Vision"

"In order to carry a positive action, we must develop here a positive vision."

- Dalai Lama

As I have written before, light comes as we work towards it. The early years of the 21st century brought opportunities to expand need-based services for blind children as well as blind people in general. Since 1976-77, the idea of introducing services for people with low vision had been strongly occupying my mind. These services were greatly needed but were not available in this region.

Dr. Ulka Shrivastava, then a lecturer in ophthalmology at MGM Medical College, was kind enough to respond to our request for a short-term visit to a low vision care center in Bombay, which was one of the key initiatives of the National Association for the Blind, India. After her visit, NAB, MP, requested the Department of Ophthalmology at MY Hospital to introduce a low vision care center as part of their need-based services. The center was inaugurated by the then Minister for Health, Government of Madhya Pradesh, and began offering regular services once a week to low vision patients under Dr. Ulka Shrivastava's supervision. NAB, MP, provided all necessary trial kits and other essential accessories for the unit.

Over time, the Madhya Pradesh Welfare Association for the Blind, Indore, also recognized the importance of such services for the community. As a result, a team of professionals was sent for short-term training at L V Prasad Eye Hospital, Hyderabad, which was the only eye center of its kind in India. Dr. Subhash Bande, Dr. Mohini Thakre, and Shri. Mahipal attended the training on behalf of the association.

After gaining the necessary expertise, a low vision care center was established at Prakash Nagar under the auspices of the MP Welfare Association for the Blind. The center operated twice a week, benefiting a significant number of patients. Low vision children, in particular, gained the ability to join regular schools and use printed materials adapted with large print.

At that time, with the dedicated efforts of Shri. Subhash Datrange, Executive Director of NAB, India, the Government of India recognized this new discipline and approved financial support for such initiatives. Consequently, nine similar projects were launched across India with government funding. This support played a crucial role in promoting visual rehabilitation, helping patients maximize their residual vision to the fullest extent.

It was then agreed in principle that the state government should take responsibility for supporting this unique unit in Madhya Pradesh. However, instead of facilitating the project, bureaucratic hurdles prevented the necessary applications from reaching the Government of India for financial assistance. As a result, the project could no longer be sustained by the organization.

***

Chapter 21

International Collaborations

"If everyone is moving forward together, then success takes care of itself."

– Chris Bradford

The activities of the MP Welfare Association for the Blind gained international recognition!

Aid-et-Action (Paris) for Education Activities

To our surprise, a representative from Aid-et-Action, a Paris-based international organization, reached out to me through Dr. Rao of the Pandit Sunderlal Sharma Central Institute of Vocational Education in Bhopal. Aid-et-Action had a regional office in Bhopal, led by its director, Mr. Kashinath, and was primarily dedicated to promoting elementary education in the region.

For the first time, the organization expressed interest in supporting an institution working for the education of blind children. After extensive discussions, Aid-et-Action agreed to fund the MP Welfare Association for the Blind's educational initiatives under the project title 'Anubhooti' for a period of five years. By then, the educational activities were being conducted under the name Helen Keller Education Academy.

The financial assistance from Aid-et-Action amounted to ₹1 crore over five years, with the following key objectives:

(a) Enhancing the quality of education through skill development.

(b) Promoting universal education by encouraging inclusive education alongside mainstream schooling.

(c) Introducing innovative, need-based educational services.

This support from Aid-et-Action was utilized to its fullest potential, successfully achieving the prescribed objectives and earning the appreciation of the funding agency.

Sense International (UK) for Deaf-Blind Children

Meanwhile, the UK-based international organization Sense International also reached out to the MP Welfare Association for the Blind, encouraging the initiation of services for deaf-blind children. Sense International is dedicated to supporting children who are both visually and hearing impaired. Their regional office in Ahmedabad had already funded 19 such projects across different parts of the country.

Not only was the organization successful in implementing this project, but it also continued providing services for nearly two years even after the official funding ended.

International agencies extend technical and financial support for a stipulated period, expecting recipient organizations to sustain the initiative through alternative resources. The vision they provide for such causes is often more valuable than the funds themselves—something many recipient organizations fail to recognize. Sustainability must be a priority from the very first day of receiving financial and technical support. This remains a crucial issue for organizations relying on foreign funding for specific projects.

Royal Commonwealth Society for the Blind (UK)

The Royal Commonwealth Society for the Blind, headquartered in the UK, has long been dedicated to the prevention of blindness and rehabilitation services. For many years, they supported initiatives in India and other Commonwealth countries to promote these causes. I had the privilege of being associated with them twice—first in 1987-88—when I secured their support for NAB, MP to conduct a Community-Based Rehabilitation (CBR) program in the Mhow block.

Over time, the organization began operating under the name Sight Savers (India). Given my background and dedicated service, along with the capable team at our disposal, Sight Savers extended financial and technical support to run a CBR project in the Depalpur block of Indore district for three years.

This project enabled blind and low-vision children, who had previously been unable to attend regular schools, to integrate into mainstream education with the necessary support. Itinerant teachers, field workers, and parental counseling services were provided to facilitate this transition. Additionally, the project ensured access to eye examinations, surgeries, blindness certification, and other government-supported programs. In some cases, vision restoration was remarkably successful.

Even after the stipulated three-year period ended, Sight Savers extended its support for another year to further strengthen inclusive education efforts.

***

Chapter 22

Shobha – My Constant Stable Support

"Never above you. Never below you. Always beside you."

—Walter Winchell

As one reaches puberty, the search for a life partner begins, influenced by various factors such as physical appearance, communication skills, attitude, aptitude, education, and personal expectations. However, marriage is not always a predictable journey— for some, it turns into an uncertain gamble where reality does not align with their desires. In such situations, the key to a harmonious life lies in the ability to adapt and accommodate, making mutual understanding and compromise essential for a lasting relationship.

Fifty years ago, Indian society was largely unaware of the abilities and potential of blind individuals. A deep-rooted stigma prevailed— the belief that a fulfilling life with a blind spouse was impossible. Most girls were hesitant to make independent decisions when it came to accepting a blind person as a life partner, often finding themselves bound by societal expectations and limitations.

In this context, my marriage was an exception. Despite my blindness, I was fortunate to have an educated spouse, Shobha, by my side. Over the past 45 years, we have built our life together through mutual adjustments, understanding, and accommodation. Over time, Shobha has developed an exceptional ability to anticipate my needs, recognize my strengths, and acknowledge my limitations. Her eyes now serve both of us, a support that brings me immense relief.

Her adaptability has played a crucial role in managing our family's needs. Despite her limited formal education, she has cultivated a deep social awareness, extending her understanding beyond our home. She has not only embraced our shared journey but has also developed a keen sensitivity to the challenges faced by others with similar disabilities, making her support invaluable in more ways than one.

We have both come to understand that life's path is often narrow, and our role is either to widen it wherever possible or to navigate it as it is. My experience has shown me that the spouse of a blind person must not only work hard but also develop a deeper understanding to support their partner.

Often, an individual's true qualities remain unnoticed in daily life, only to emerge in critical moments. In times of emergency, even those with limited formal education can display remarkable strength, sometimes surpassing the so-called educated members of the family. I have witnessed this firsthand when urgent care was needed for hospitalized family members. In such situations, my life partner stepped forward with unwavering dedication, ensuring that the necessary support was provided. These experiences have reinforced my belief that sensitivity and compassion are not always tied to education—sometimes, those with fewer formal qualifications rise to the occasion when it matters most.

A supportive social environment can bring about significant changes in a person's attitude and behavior. This transformation has been evident in my life partner. Her parents were astonished to see how much she has grown in both skill and confidence. She has become more socially engaged and now feels uneasy if I am left alone, even for a few hours. As a result, I always keep her by my side, whether at home or at work. This constant companionship has given her many opportunities to meet new people, and she now actively seeks to build friendships. Additionally, her improved communication skills have strengthened her connections with relatives and friends, expanding her social circle even further.

She has always been eager to explore new places. Over the years, she has traveled to Nepal, Kashmir, Vaishnodevi, Somnath, Chitrakoot, Rameshwaram, Kanyakumari, Mumbai, Pune, Jabalpur, and several other destinations, embracing each journey with enthusiasm.

Given my health and advancing age, she has become even more attentive to my needs, responding with remarkable promptness. I see how she has gradually adapted to my way of life, aligning herself with my values and expectations. Our family life has evolved through numerous social experiences, guided by patience and a willingness to embrace change until the desired outcomes unfold.

It is essential to cultivate sensitivity in recognizing the hidden potential of those around us. By making conscious efforts in our daily lives, we can uncover the strengths of our family members and the people we interact with, fostering a more meaningful and harmonious existence.

***

Chapter 23

Inclusive Mindset Towards the Blind

"We are trying to construct a more inclusive society. We are going to make a country in which no one is left out".

– Franklin Roosevelt

People, in general—even the educated ones—often hold misconceptions about blindness. These misunderstandings lead to irrational behavior, sometimes humiliating blind individuals and fostering resentment towards those without disabilities. This, in turn, hinders the development of a harmonious relationship between blind individuals and the rest of society.

A truly inclusive society, which is the cornerstone of national progress, must cultivate sensitivity toward all groups, regardless of their limitations. To achieve this, it is essential that awareness of government-provided facilities, rules, and regulations reaches blind individuals at every level, ensuring equal access and eliminating any biases that may persist within the community.

One of the eminent educators of the blind at the international level has stated that blindness itself is not the major issue; rather, it is the attitude of society and the inadequate knowledge of professionals that turn blindness into a complex problem.

Its true that parents care and love their child much more, especially if the child has some disability. But its heart breaking that relatives in the family do not take enough interest in the wellbeing and all-round development of blind children in the family, often assuming that spending on their education will be in vain. For over a century, the education of blind children has largely been treated as a charity issue, with the assumption that their welfare is solely the responsibility of society and the government. This mindset needs to be changed urgently, and the collective efforts of enlightened educators, social workers, and administrators must be accelerated to foster a more proactive approach.

I firmly believe that family members should create a supportive environment to foster the growth and development of a blind child in the following ways:

They should behave with him or her at par of other normal members of the family. They should neither overprotect nor neglect them in all possible activities in family and relations.

If congenital blindness is identified within six months of age then early medical intervention should not be ignored rather assured.

It should be kept in mind that the development of a blind child is possible only with full social inclusion. Therefore, the child should be encouraged to sit with normal children in Anganwadi and pre-primary classes. Anganwadi workers and teachers, along with the normal children, will get the opportunity to develop awareness and skills for interacting with blind children and managing healthy behaviour within the entire system.

They should take blind child with them to attend all social functions, temples, garden, shopping, etc. Now a days, special teachers for the blind are available and their early intervention in the all-round development of blind child has become imperative for the healthy personality development of the child concerned. All family members, need to be updated with knowledge and technique, which may enable them to make all- round development of the blind child at par of his normal peers.

They should maintain resource file containing all possible relevant information about model school for blind, senior professionals in the field, organizations of the blind at national level, possible career courses, literature in the field of blind, eminent veteran, blind professionals, who could be considered as model for the generation ahead be enlisted in the resource file. Moreover, parents should take opportunity to share views with such people seeking their guidance consistent to the attitude and aptitude of the blind child concerned enabling them to make goal planning at appropriate time. Blind child be given opportunity to meet with model professionals enabling him to seek his base from them time to time.

There are also instances where blind individuals are more highly qualified than other members of their families, and in some cases, they earn more than others. It has long been assumed that educated blind youths primarily work in teaching positions, but this has changed dramatically. Blind individuals are now making strides in a variety of careers. For example, law graduates who are blind are now practicing law in High Courts and the Supreme Court. Barrister Sudhanchandra Roy even served as Advocate General for the West Bengal Government, and Mr. Damodar Wadegaonkar worked as Principal of the Government Law College in Mumbai. This shift is a testament to the growing opportunities for blind individuals in diverse professions.

In recent years, a growing number of blind male and female youths have seized opportunities in various fields, including banking, where some have ascended to senior positions such as Branch Manager and General Manager. Perhaps most remarkably, a few blind intellectuals have successfully cleared the Indian Administrative Services (IAS) exams and are now holding prestigious positions within the government.

This is the right time for society to dispel the myth that knowledge is primarily acquired through sight. The residual senses, the power of the mind, and inner will can overcome the so-called limitations often associated with blindness. A powerful example of this is a blind youth, 23 years old, who recently scored an impressive 97% and secured the first position in M.Sc. (Mathematics) at the Indian Institute of Technology (IIT) Kharagpur. This single achievement shatters the belief that the loss of sight equates to the loss of potential.

These examples serve as a compelling reminder of the need to develop a rational, inclusive vision regarding blindness. I hope that readers will share these realistic and inspiring stories with their friends, helping to further the cause of social inclusion for blind people across all occupations.

***

Chapter 24

Life is Divine – Embrace it!

"Your vision will become clear only when you can look into your own heart. Who looks outside, dreams; who looks inside, awakes."

- Carl Jung

Most of us perceive life as an intricate puzzle, dedicating our energy, interests, and material resources to solving it. Some succeed in their efforts, and a select few emerge as guiding lights—friends, philosophers, and mentors—whose wisdom continues to inspire future generations. Their innovative approaches shape lives, fostering happiness and progress.

Vision for divine life, as explained by Swami Shivanandaji, does not require eyesight. Rather, the misty veil of ignorance can be removed, and enlightenment can dawn through contemplation and meditation. This requires a different vision inherent within the self, which should be strengthened continuously through contemplation and meditation. Children should be motivated by their parents to engage in contemplation until they reach puberty.

At that point, the younger generation becomes capable of directing their contemplation in the right direction.

Everyone must be exposed to spiritual literature based on their age, educational level, and mental development. I highly recommend the book 'Inspirational Thoughts' by Swami Shivananda. This book contains invaluable spiritual wisdom such as:-

(a) **The Meaning and Message of Life:** Understanding the purpose of life leads to true happiness. By not chasing materialistic pleasures at the expense of values, one finds lasting fulfillment and maintains faith in difficult times.

(b) **The Voice of Conscience:** The conscience, though often clouded by desires and guilt, contains pure wisdom when listened to. The inner voice is the voice of God, guiding us to make choices aligned with truth and goodness.

(c) **Be Yourself:** Authenticity is key to a peaceful and successful life. Pretending to be someone else leads to eventual disappointment, while being true to oneself fosters inner peace and respect.

(d) **The Goal and the Path:** When you are certain that your mission is just, pursue it relentlessly with patience and dedication. Know your limits and move forward with resolve and perseverance.

(e) **Work for Self-satisfaction:** Act according to your inner voice, prioritizing self-satisfaction over external approval. Listen carefully to your conscience and let it guide your actions for a balanced and peaceful life.

(f) **Move in the Positive Direction:** Confidence and hope lead to success. Recognizing and nurturing your unique talents, while addressing your weaknesses with patience, brings growth and fulfillment.

(g) **No Shortcut to Success:** Success comes through consistent effort and overcoming challenges. Replace negative emotions with positive qualities, and have faith in the Divine for guidance.

(h) **Part and Yet Apart:** While we are all part of society, each individual is unique. Understanding both the common aspects of human nature and individual differences allows for better interpersonal relationships and personal growth.

(i) **Surrender to the Divine:** Surrendering is not about giving up your identity but expanding your consciousness and aligning with the Divine. This leads to inner peace, strength, and bliss, allowing you to live harmoniously with the world.

Human life is the most precious gift given to us, and it should not be wasted at any cost. The mysteries of life are revealed to those who keep their minds awake at all times. Life is real, life is earnest, and the grave is not its goal. Life is a powerful flame, and we live by an invisible Sun within us.

An aimless life is always a miserable life. It matters not how long we live, but how we live. Live with a specific aim and strive to achieve it. Contemplate and enjoy it as a divine gift, and allow others to share in it. A good life is a happy life. It does not mean that being good will make you happy; rather, if you are happy, you are good.

Life is a great school in which you are constantly learning how to work, plan, and achieve as long as you live. As long as you live, keep learning how to live life. Life can only be understood in hindsight, but it must be lived forwards. We are born crying, live complaining, and die disappointed. That is why it is said that how narrow is the path that leads to life, and how broad is the road that leads to destruction. Hence, we must concentrate our efforts to widen the path that leads to life. Remember, life is a tragedy for those who feel and a comedy for those who think. God is the greatest architect of the universe, where millions of people and innumerable creatures survive. However, no two people are alike. Thus, man's life is a fairy tale written by God's fingers.

***

Chapter 25

Golden Values for a Happy Life

"If you want to be happy, set a goal that commands your thoughts, liberates your energy, and inspires your hopes."

— Andrew Carnegie

Everyone wants to enjoy a happy life, but the idea of how to attain happiness varies from person to person. It depends on one's cultural background, attitude, aptitude, and personal philosophy of life. There is no one specific way to lead a happy and fulfilling life.

I believe that if a person's values are set right, they lay the foundation for a happy life.

During childhood, parents and family members play a vital role in shaping a child's values, which influence the course of their life. Values like positive thinking, politeness, respect for elders, love for the younger generation, and compassion for animals and nature form the foundation of a well-rounded character.

Here are some priceless golden values, which have personally led me to a happy and fulfilling life:

Value 1: Following One's Religion

Children should be given ample opportunity to embrace faith, while ensuring they are not exposed to atheism. We all believe that God helps those who help themselves. Faith in religion and the almighty helps regulate our minds, tempering them in a positive direction. Children should be nurtured from an early age with these concepts, which will help strengthen their inner will. Gradually, this leads to the development of self-confidence and positive action.

Small handbooks on theism and religion should be made available to children, helping them develop an interest in these life values through literature.

A common group prayer should be introduced in each family at a specific time every day. With a conducive environment, this practice will become spontaneous for every family member. Over time, this practice will charge the family's harmonics, enhancing the productivity of each individual in a positive direction. It is often experienced in families where common prayer is practiced daily that they enjoy a pleasant and prosperous life. Opportunities to overcome even complex problems arise, and positive solutions emerge naturally.

Value 2: Hard work

Hard work in the right direction, under the guidance of experienced mentors, brings desired results. Focus on one task at a time with full dedication, and once positive results are achieved, only then take on the next mission at hand.

Value 3: Honesty

One must have sincere intentions in pursuing a noble purpose and be honest in his/her ways in achieving the same.

Value 4: Perseverance

One must cultivate strong willpower to persevere on the path to their purpose, which is filled with obstacles.

Thus, having the above values can guide individuals towards personal growth, happiness, and spiritual fulfillment.

***

Chapter 26

Seeing the Unseen Horizons

"You cannot swim for new horizons until you have courage to lose sight of the shore."

— William Faulkner

The title of this book carries a deep and inherent significance. I firmly believe that vision is far more profound and essential for human perfection than mere eyesight. While it is widely assumed that 80% of knowledge is acquired through sight, I find this notion to be vague and debatable. When eyesight is lost, all other sensory organs continue to function as channels of understanding, allowing an individual to perceive the world through heightened awareness.

A person who loses eyesight must maximize the potential of their residual senses, making them not disabled but truly "differently abled". Recognizing this, the term 'Differently Abled People' is gaining global acceptance, reflecting a more accurate and empowering perspective. Beyond sensory perception, memory and experience play a crucial role in shaping one's personality and intellect.

History offers remarkable examples of blind individuals whose contributions have transformed society. A blind pianist in the United States pioneered the concept of a typewriter based on touch. The Postmaster General of the United Kingdom, despite being blind, introduced the money order system. It is also believed that the study of honeybees, which led to advancements in beekeeping science, was initiated by a blind researcher.

All of the above examples indicate the major role of the mind and the sense of creativity in any innovation. This has nothing to do with eyesight. I am not underestimating the role of eyesight; however, one should not overemphasize eyesight and ignore other inherent faculties and senses that nature has bestowed upon each of us. Whether we have sight or not, the contributions of people without eyesight have spread all over the world in various fields such as poetry, literature, culture, science, politics, and more. Inner vision, as I have experienced throughout my life, is an ongoing process that is acquired and developed gradually through knowledge, experience, adaptability, and, above all, the blessings of nature.

I have observed that many times, people with eyesight do not pay attention to the vision we gain through residual senses and other faculties. This adversely affects the human development process, and that loss cannot be measured by any means. Vision comes as we work for it; sometimes, it does not come through residual senses. The real and lasting vision one may attain is only experienced through inner will, and when it is extended to others, it becomes a driving force for all those who preserve it as an eternal sense.

Sharing these hidden realities of life, I have a note of caution for blind people: in general, they cannot survive without the support of sighted individuals. Throughout their lives, they acquire knowledge by borrowing eyesight from sighted people, relying on them almost every moment, and constantly seeking help for one thing or another. Here, it is essential for blind individuals to remain positive and cordial when seeking help, maintaining harmonious and healthy relationships with those around them. Dr. Helen Keller achieved remarkable feats and became a unique woman of the world. While acknowledging this reality, we must not overlook the contributions of Annie Sullivan, Tara Fullar, Polly Thompson, and many other sighted individuals who supported a deaf-blind child and helped her reach such high stature. This serves as a notable example of how dedicated sighted individuals have helped multiply disabled persons, making them wonders of the world.

Swami Vivekananda, Swami Dayananda, and many other thinkers made substantial contributions to human society, not merely through their sight, but through the vision they received from the supreme power of Almighty God. Even Dr. Helen Keller once said, *"Utmost real beauty cannot be seen nor even experienced by residual senses, but one gets it through his or her inner will, and that is called real vision."*

In the field of the Mahabharata, Lord Krishna preached to Arjun about human life, karma yoga, dedication, and much more. This has become a lasting vision for the entire human community, which will inspire generations to come to understand the vision that is everlasting for the universe. That vision must be nurtured throughout one's life if one wishes to contribute something substantial to society for its wellbeing. Shrimad Bhagwat Geeta is not meant to be read by eyesight alone, but to be internalized through the inner will to regulate our behavior and actions. That is why Shrimad Bhagwat Geeta has now become an adopted handbook of practice for every individual across the world.

***

Epilogue

"Create the highest, grandest vision possible for your life, because you become, what you believe."

-Oprah Winfrey

As an orphan who had also lost sight, my life initially seemed destined for darkness—both literally and figuratively. I was at the mercy of Mother Nature, lacking the guidance and security that many others take for granted. Yet, I have never believed that nature or providence was cruel to me. On the contrary, I was gifted with unique strengths—an inner vision that allowed me to see beyond my disability. That is where the philosophy of my life began to take shape, born from hardship but nurtured by an unshakable will.

It was willpower alone that steered me toward positive thinking, and from there, assertive action. I embarked on my life's journey with nothing but the determination to overcome challenges. Gradually, this mindset led me to discover solutions for even the most difficult situations. Positive thinking and decisive action became the foundation of my life, guiding me toward a path of purpose. Over time, this philosophy evolved into a driving force behind my contributions to social welfare, allowing me to turn adversity into an opportunity for collective growth.

During my youth, while pursuing my education in Mumbai, I was fortunate to experience a rich social environment and meaningful exposure to influential personalities. I had the honor of welcoming and interacting with international icons such as Dr. Helen Keller, as well as eminent national leaders like Prime Minister Pt. Jawaharlal Nehru and Shri. Morarji Desai. Their philosophies left an enduring impact on my outlook and aspirations. These encounters shaped the foundation of my life's philosophy—where hard work, commitment, and service became guiding principles, leading me toward a life of purpose and contribution.

Economic independence is the foundation of meaningful service to others. Recognizing this, I made employment and self-reliance—not just for myself but for others—a central pursuit in my life's journey. However, I never allowed myself to become obsessed with accumulating wealth for personal gain.

Looking back, I realize that my passive attitude toward financial stability in the past was not entirely fair to my future self. The consequences of this approach have surfaced in later years, but I do not view them with regret. Sacrifices are inevitable for those who aspire to achieve higher goals in service of society. Some personal comforts may have been forsaken, but the larger purpose I pursued continues to give my life meaning and fulfillment.

The thirst for knowledge has been a defining force in my life since childhood. Even with poor eyesight until the age of 14, I immersed myself in books on the independence movement and the lives of patriots who sacrificed everything for the nation. Losing my sight temporarily disrupted my education, but I refused to let it end there.

With perseverance, I resumed my studies and continued them alongside my job and voluntary work. At 36, I earned my master's degree in sociology—all while serving as the Honorary Secretary of the MP Welfare Association for the Blind in Indore. I aspired to pursue a PhD, but circumstances did not allow me to complete it. However, my commitment to learning has never wavered, and it continues to shape my journey.

A short-term training in rehabilitation counseling in USA sparked my interest in clinical psychology, allowing me to understand human behavior, its underlying causes, and possible ways to regulate it. This knowledge proved invaluable in my interactions with people, helping me offer guidance and support where needed.

I admit that I am a bit oversensitive to human suffering. Whenever someone comes to me seeking relief, I feel an innate urge to help. This deep empathy has shaped my approach to life, reinforcing my commitment to serving others in any way I can.

I grew up in unique socio-economic conditions that shaped my personality, steering me away from self-centered pursuits. My experiences instilled in me a deep sense of social responsibility, compelling me to focus on the collective good rather than personal gain.

As I reflect on my journey, I leave it to the discerning readers of this autobiography to assess whether there were any deviations or unintended elements that may have influenced my life's mission. If such instances occurred, they were never intentional but rather part of the complex fabric of human experience.

Now, at the age of 83 I have withdrawn from active social service. Society recognized my humble contributions with admiration and appreciation. I stepped back to allow the successors to carry the mission forward more vigorously, in line with the changing needs and the new advantages available to them.

Now I like to spend time in creative writing. Fortunately, I am working with Shri. Prakash Trivedi, an experienced stenographer, who has been instrumental in bringing this creative writing endeavor to life. He worked with me for several years as a staff member of the MP Welfare Association for the Blind. I found him to be the most suitable person to support my creative writing goals, as his dedication to my mission reflects the drive needed to turn this long-held dream into a reality.

Throughout these years, my focus was primarily on social action, with my life partner always by my side, supporting and driving these programs forward. Neither of us had the opportunity to enjoy a relaxed and comfortable life over these 45 years. Therefore, visiting pilgrimages and historic places has become a special focus for us. At this stage, maintaining good health despite the limitations of aging is equally important. As such, I now dedicate considerable time each day to yoga, exercise, diet planning, and recreation.

I could never truly indulge in a specific hobby throughout my life, as social action itself became my sole passion. However, these days, I take time to enjoy listening to good songs on Vividh Bharati and engage in group discussions and lectures on current topics. I have always had a deep curiosity about staying informed on current affairs, and this habit has remained a ritual for me.

In recent years, I have grown more inclined towards nurturing my inner vision, connecting with nature, drawing on spiritual strength, and recognizing the power of the divine in those around me.

I have battled with insomnia for many years, requiring sedative medicines for an extended period. But to my surprise, as I've relaxed and freed myself from worry, I now enjoy sound sleep—not just at night, but I also take a nap each day, lasting about an hour.

I have developed an interest in counseling on selected issues, particularly those that help improve family dynamics, and I offer consultations to parents of disabled children, where they find my advice to be realistic and resourceful.

In a true sense, I am now fully embracing the stage of Vaanprashth ashram, and I believe my life partner is experiencing a similar sense of fulfillment at this stage of life.

The essence of my life has taught me, with utmost humility, that every positive step taken with an assertive approach toward a common goal eventually brings us closer to true fulfillment. There is no greater joy than the lasting pleasure that comes from alleviating the struggles of others, for in their relief, we find our own.

***